HANGOVER
HELPER

LAUREN SHOCKEY

For Ross

**THERE'S NO ONE I'D RATHER
BE HUNGOVER WITH THAN YOU**

HANGOVER HELPER

DELICIOUS CURES FROM AROUND THE WORLD
LAUREN SHOCKEY

Hardie Grant

BOOKS

CHAPTER 1

BOOZY AND VIRGIN BEVERAGES 27

CHAPTER 2

ALL ABOUT EGGS 57

CHEERS!

PROST!

S

KANPAI!

Whether you're downing icy shots of neat vodka at a Russian *dacha*, sipping on Mai Tais on the sunny shores of Hawaii's Waikiki Beach or knocking back pints of Japanese craft beer in five-seater bars in Tokyo's Golden Gai, the clinking of goblets, flutes and coupes is globally synonymous with merriment.

You know what's also universal? The unbearable hangover that inevitably follows. Indeed, whether you hail from London or Las Vegas, São Paulo or Seoul, whether you're young or old, rich or poor, male or female, a daiquiri drinker or a Tanqueray tippler, hangovers do not discriminate. We may all be a little too familiar with the

manifestation of unpleasant physical and mental symptoms that occur after a round of heavy drinking: nausea, headache, dizziness, fatigue, dry mouth, general malaise and the urge to spend the rest of the day under the covers. But what exactly *is* a hangover?

The scourge of the morning after usually begins the night before. Hangovers emerge within a few hours of paying the bar tab, as your blood alcohol level begins to fall. Symptoms then usually peak around the time your blood alcohol reaches zero (that's to say, roughly when you wake up) and can continue for up to 24 hours thereafter – or even longer, if you're the poor

SALUTE!

ANTÉ!

bloke from Scotland who holds the world record of having a four-week-long hangover after drinking 60 pints over a four-day bender. Yet given the many physiological variables at play, we still don't understand exactly how hangovers inflict their misery.

What we do know is that alcohol is a diuretic and causes the body to increase its urinary output. This, along with the sweating and vomiting that can occur alongside a hangover, often results in fluid loss, electrolyte imbalances, weakness and general dehydration. But that's not the whole story. Anyone who's chugged a few glasses of water after a bender knows that despite your foresight,

you might still wake with a pounding headache. Indeed, research has indicated that a hangover and dehydration are two independent yet co-occurring processes.

Alcohol also causes gastritis, an inflammation of the stomach lining, which may account for some of the tummy-churning feelings you have when hungover. And while alcohol might put you right to bed, booze-induced sleep is usually of a shorter duration than normal, and of worse quality than what you're used to, which contributes to fatigue and sluggishness the following day.

100%

GUARANTEED WAY TO AVOID HANGOVERS IS TO ABSTAIN FROM DRINKING IN THE FIRST PLACE

What's more, your body breaks down alcohol into some nasty chemicals known to cause nausea, and these trigger most of the stomach-achy effects of drinking one too many. Additionally, low blood sugar may contribute to feeling terrible, but then again, a hangover could also be an inflammatory response. Or the culprit might be acute alcohol withdrawal, suggesting – falsely – that what you really need is a tad more alcohol to balance you out.

Which boils down to one thing ... we still don't know how to prevent hangovers. Indeed, a survey of the academic literature on hangovers has determined that there is no irrefutable evidence to suggest that any specific remedy is truly effective.

Rather, the only tried and true, 100 per cent guaranteed way to avoid hangovers is to abstain from drinking in the first place. But where's the fun in that? Total abstinence would mean turning your back on the rich and varied history of making – and indulging in – wine, beer and spirits.

Before our ancestors planted food, discovered fire or even communicated in a spoken language, early humans were consuming alcohol. True, early indulgences likely took the form of chomping into half-rotten oranges found on the jungle floor rather than downing pints at the Red Lion's happy hour, but we can still safely assume that people got tipsy. And as long as we've been getting drunk, we've been getting hangovers.

BUT WHERE'S THE FUN IN THAT?

And as long as we've been getting hangovers, we've been searching for effective – and enticing – remedies.

The oldest record of a culinary hangover cure dates all the way back to the 10th century, found in Ibn Sayyar al-Warraq's tome of 600 recipes entitled *Kitab al-Tabīh*. He includes a recipe for an Iraqi meat stew called *kishkiyya*, made by combining meat, chickpeas, warming spices and *kashk*, a mixture of fermented yoghurt, milk and whey. A bowl of it, says al-Warraq, will revive you and cure the ills of your hangover.

He might have been on to something. Hearty, meaty stews still reign supreme as hangover fare around the world, from South Korea to Turkey to Bolivia. But this wasn't always the case. Ancient Egyptians believed in curing hangovers by wearing wreaths of Alexandrian *chamaedaphne*, a laurel-like shrub. Aristotle suggested eating cabbage leaves, while the Roman philosopher Pliny the Elder endorsed eating fried canaries (in Pliny's defence, this was 19 centuries before Colonel Sanders would establish chicken as the favourite fried fowl of over-indulgers). In the Middle Ages, raw eel was a popular treatment, while John of Gaddesden's 14th century medical treatise, *Rosa Medicinae*, advised washing one's testicles or breasts in vinegar.

Fortunately, today's hangover remedies are a bit more accessible and a lot more delicious. Egg dishes are popular in many Western countries, as is greasy, carb-heavy food. Soups and stews, meanwhile, are beloved in South America and much of Asia. Salty, savoury dishes are much more common on the breakfast table the morning after than anything sugary; very few countries boast of sweet hangover saviours. Sandwiches are widespread across the globe, likely because they're fast and filling, and, let's get real – you can eat them in bed. Spicy foods, believed to help sweat out the toxins, are touted far and wide. 'Wellness' foods and beverages are gaining in popularity as the self-care craze has taken hold. And a little 'hair of the dog' has long been seen as a trusty way of getting through the day. Okay, maybe a lot of it.

Folklore and mythmaking also have a hand in promoting hangover cures. Do Sicilians really eat *pizzle* (otherwise known as dried bull penis)? Do Mongolians actually slurp down pickled sheep's eyeballs in tomato juice (jokingly referred to as a Mongolian Mary)? Evidence points otherwise, but there's something endlessly fascinating about the extreme lengths folks will go to cure a hangover.

This book explores the many delicious ways in which the world recovers from a night out. However, let me assure you that having a hangover is by no means a requirement for enjoying the recipes that follow – this is just as much a book for armchair travellers and teetotallers as it is for world-weary tipplers. I promise you that the recipes taste just as good stone-cold sober as they do hungover. Nevertheless, I've made them both craveable and easy to prepare when your head is throbbing and all you want to do is go back to bed. Hence

you won't find a recipe for sheep's head soup or plantains in offal sauce in the pages here, even though those are celebrated hangover cures in Tehran and Kampala, respectively.

As the diversity of the recipes illustrates, no single food is guaranteed to rid you of your hangover completely. Likewise, one man's killer hangover may be another's everyday headache, and the hangover you have today may feel completely different to the one you had two weeks ago. Hangover characteristics may depend on what, exactly, you drink, and how much you drink of it, meaning it's difficult to replicate the same hangover day-to-day. You may crave a plate full of carbs one day and a simple broth the next. Just as there is not one defining cause of a hangover, there is not one single magic culinary cure-all.

Hopefully, the dishes featured in this book will help alleviate some combination of your nausea, fatigue, chills and ills; if they don't, at least drink plenty of water, possibly pop an ibuprofen or two, and take a nap. The good thing about a terrible hangover is that it will, with time and rest, eventually go away. So, go ahead, clink those glasses and enjoy one more round. Even if you end up *futsukayoi* (or 'two days drunk' as the Japanese say) with *une gueule de bois* ('a mouth of wood', a French term for hangover), at least you know you've got a little help to get you through the next day.

WORDS OF
WISDOM

You don't need to drink to excess to be witty ... but it doesn't hurt. Here are some famous hangover quips from celebrated authors, poets and musicians.

THE ONLY
REAL CURE FOR
A HANGOVER
IS DEATH.

Robert Benchley

I FEEL BAD FOR PEOPLE
WHO DON'T DRINK. WHEN
THEY WAKE UP IN THE
MORNING, THAT'S AS
GOOD AS THEY'RE GOING
TO FEEL ALL DAY.

Frank Sinatra

ALWAYS DO SOBER WHAT
YOU SAID YOU'D DO DRUNK.
THAT WILL TEACH YOU TO
KEEP YOUR MOUTH SHUT.

Ernest Hemingway

IF GETTING DRUNK WAS HOW PEOPLE FORGOT THEY WERE MORTAL, THEN HANGOVERS WERE HOW THEY REMEMBERED.

from *The Humans*, Matt Haig

A HANGOVER IS THE WRATH OF GRAPES.

Dorothy Parker

DON'T TRUST A BRILLIANT IDEA UNLESS IT SURVIVES THE HANGOVER.

Jimmy Breslin

HIS HEAD WAS POUNDING AND HIS VISION SKEWED IN SOME WAY AND HE WAS VAGUELY AMAZED AT BEING ALIVE AND NOT SURE THAT IT WAS WORTH IT.

from *Suttree*, Cormac McCarthy

GLOBAL DRINKING STATS AND FIGURES

Drinkers can be found in nearly every corner of the globe, though some regions of the world enjoy hitting the bottle a bit more than others. According to data from the World Health Organization, Europe – and Eastern Europe in particular – is home to some of the world's champion boozers. Per capita alcohol consumption in both Moldova and Lithuania clocks in at about a whopping 15 litres (4 gallons) a year, which equates to about a shot a day. Needless to say, that's a lot of hangovers. Unsurprisingly, the countries with the lowest per capita consumption are mostly found in the Middle East as well as in other Muslim-majority countries such as Niger and Indonesia, where alcohol is frowned upon or forbidden.

45%

of all the alcohol that we chug comes in the form of spirits (think vodka, whisky, gin, etc.)

34%

comes from beer.

12%

from wine.

The remaining 9 per cent comes from other types of alcohol and fermented beverages.

HOW TO AVOID A HANGOVER IN THE FIRST PLACE

Food the next day may be your saving grace, but here are some helpful hints for minimising a hangover's impact in the first place:

CHUG LOTS OF WATER

while drinking and before heading to bed. Keep a glass of H_2O on your nightstand to quench your thirst when you wake with a dry mouth at 4 a.m.

KNOW AND RESPECT YOUR LIMITS

when it comes to drinking. Better yet, opt for a mocktail. It's a sure-fire way to avoid a hangover!

DRAW THE SHADES

A study found recuperating in total darkness to be effective in reducing a hangover's recovery time.

CUT OUT THE CIGS

Smoking significantly increases the odds of getting a hangover and makes them more severe.

BE A HAPPY, OPTIMISTIC DRUNK!

Negative life events, neuroticism, being angry when drunk and having feelings of guilt about drinking are also associated with experiencing more hangovers.

ENJOY A HEARTY MEAL

prior to drinking. Carb- and fat-heavy foods will help slow alcohol's absorption in the body.

GO EASY ON THE BUBBLY

The carbon dioxide in sparkling wines and other fizzy alcoholic drinks speeds up the alcohol's absorption in your body faster than beverages without bubbles.

CHOOSE LIGHTER-COLOURED DRINKS

like gin, vodka, beer and white wine. Darker drinks (e.g. bourbon, brandy, red wine, etc.) contain higher levels of congeners, which can contribute to hangovers.

AND REMEMBER, YOU CAN'T BE HUNGOVER IF YOU'RE STILL DRUNK!

ABOUT THAT HEARTY MEAL WHILE DRINKING ...

You might consider drunk food and hangover food to be one and the same, and, indeed, many dishes (hello, poutine!) straddle both culinary genres. While hangover meals are generally about self-love, drunk food is purely about self-lust. Drunk food is the id to hangover food's superego. Drunk food should also follow a few basic principles:

- It ought to be generally unhealthy due to its high carb and/or fat content. A salad is not drunk food.
- It must be inexpensive because you likely won't remember eating it the next day. Foie gras is not drunk food.

- It should be easily transportable and can preferably be eaten with one hand on your walk home from the pub. A plate of steak and mash is not drunk food.
- Drunk food is likely street food, or comes from a takeaway rather than something prepared at home. And, perhaps, it might even help in preventing the following day's hangover.

So before indulging in some global hangover cures, be sure to try some of these drunk food favourites from around the world:

ENGLAND
Doner kebabs

UNITED STATES
Pizza by the slice

GERMANY
Currywurst (a sliced sausage doused in ketchup, sprinkled with curry powder)

SCOTLAND
Munchy box (a pizza box filled with an assortment of foods that may include kebab meat, pizza, onion rings, fried rice, French fries, Chinese noodles, coleslaw, chicken tikka, ribs, chicken wings, naan and more)

PORTUGAL
Bifana (a sandwich of thinly sliced pork marinated in garlic and white wine in a crusty roll)

INDIA
Mutton or chicken roll

SOUTH KOREA
Tteokbokki (stir-fried chewy rice cakes in a spicy chilli sauce)

UGANDA
A *rolex* (no, not the watch! It's a chapati filled with scrambled eggs and vegetables)

MEXICO
Tacos

FINLAND
Lihapiirakka (a sort of savoury doughnut stuffed with minced (ground) meat)

TURKEY
Kokoreç (grilled lamb intestines chopped and stuffed into a sandwich)

POLAND
Zapiekanka (half a baguette topped with sliced mushrooms and melted cheese, plus optional toppings such as ketchup)

OTHER GLOBAL HANGOVER CURES

Don't feel like turning on the oven? There are several other ways to help ease a hangover that don't involve cooking.

SWEAT IT OUT!

Hop in a sauna to sweat it all out (especially loved throughout Scandinavia).

GET AN IV DRIP

Most common in nightlife-centric cities like New Orleans and Los Angeles.

TRY A POLAR BEAR SWIM

Jumping into ice-cold ocean waters, especially on New Year's Day, is popular in coastal cities such as Vancouver, New York, Annapolis, Busan and Scheveningen.

HIT UP AN OXYGEN BAR

Though the efficacy of this is debatable, you'll find these bars in hard-partying places like Las Vegas as well as in many mountainous areas.

A FEW NOTES ON INGREDIENTS

SALT

All salt listed is for sea salt flakes (kosher salt), which have larger crystals than table salt. If you only have table salt, use slightly less than whatever the recipe calls for. And, as with all cooking, always taste as you go along, adjusting the seasoning to your liking.

BUTTER

All butter listed is for unsalted butter, unless specifically noted in the recipe. Unsalted butter is better for cooking as you have more control over the salt flavours of your food. But again, if you only have salted butter in the house, that's fine; just use less salt than what the recipe calls for.

MILK

All milk listed is full-fat (whole) milk. If you don't have full-fat milk, you should still be fine using semi-skimmed or skimmed. Almond milk and oat milk are delicious with cereal or coffee, but probably won't work as well in most of these recipes.

FLOUR

All flour listed is plain (all-purpose). The recipes have not been tested with any other flours (for example, wholemeal (whole wheat) flour, rice flour, bread flour, etc.), so if you want to use those, proceed at your own risk (but let me know how they turn out!).

SPECIALTY INGREDIENTS

A few of the recipes in this book call for specialty ingredients that you might not find at your local supermarket. The beauty of today's world is that even if you live in the smallest of towns, you can easily order these items on the internet. I've noted in the ingredient list where something hard to procure is optional, but as you're delving into the world of global hangover food, why not check out an Asian, Latin or Eastern European supermarket and stock up on some unfamiliar ingredients? Who knows what more deliciousness you might uncover!

A GUIDE TO THE RECIPES

In addition to the estimated prep and cooking times, next to each of the recipes in this book, you'll find a handy symbol indicating the relative level of difficulty a hungover person would face when preparing each dish.

EASY TO MAKE HUNGOVER

Simply put, you should have no trouble preparing these dishes and drinks, no matter what state you find yourself in come morning (or mid-afternoon, as the case may be). Most of these recipes take less than 15 minutes to make and require minimal, if any, cooking.

A LITTLE CHALLENGING TO MAKE HUNGOVER

These recipes do take some level of clear-headedness, and you will need to either fire up the hob or turn on the oven. The prep work for these dishes isn't that bad, though, and you should be able to power through your headache. That said, if you've got a flatmate or significant other to whom you can outsource some of the chopping while you rest in bed another 15 minutes, maybe that's not that bad of an idea.

DIFFICULT TO MAKE HUNGOVER

These recipes are difficult for a variety of reasons. A few of them are a challenge because they are slow cooked, so the start-to-finish time may be a few hours (if this is too daunting or you simply don't want to wait that long for lunch, know that you can prepare most of them the night before and reheat them the following day). A recipe may also be deemed difficult because even though the cooking time is short, you need to use three different pots and pans (washing up is part of the cooking process, too, after all!). A recipe may also fall into this category because it requires you to deep-fry or use a mandoline, potentially scary kitchen endeavours even when you're not hungover. You may not want to attempt these recipes when your head is banging and your stomach is turning like a washing machine on the final spin cycle. But remember, just because something is designated as hangover food, doesn't mean you can only enjoy it when you're hurting. Many of these dishes make for great snacks, weekday dinners and Sunday suppers alike.

Perhaps one day you'll find yourself hungover in a foreign country in need of some food. When your skull's pounding, head to the closest restaurant and utter the magic words 'I'm hungover' in the native language, and hopefully someone will appear bearing plates of soul-warming, head-fixing food. Here are a few translations to keep handy:

Swedish
JAG ÄR BAKIS

Italian
HO I POSTUMI DELLA SBORNIA

Spanish (Mexico)
ESTOY CRUDO

Spanish (Ecuador)
ESTOY CHUCHAQUI

Portuguese
ESTOU DE RESSACA

Polish
MAM KACA

German
ICH BIN VERKATERT

Dutch
IK HEB EEN KATER

Hungarian
MÁSNAPOS VAGYOK

CHAPTER 1

BOOZY AND VIRGIN BEVERAGES

Your doctor will tell you that drinking alcohol when hungover isn't a bright idea because hitting the bottle will only dehydrate you more. That may technically be true, but any person who's had some 'hair of the dog' (that's to say, a bit of the booze that got you into trouble in the first place) will counter that it seemingly works wonders in lifting the dense fog surrounding your head. If the mere thought of ingesting anything alcoholic when hungover makes you shudder, try the non-boozy sips instead to alleviate your ills. From warming teas to quirky, down-the-hatch, alcohol-free shots, you'll soon be hydrated and happy (or at least less miserable) in no time.

PICKLE BRINE BLOODY MARY

USA BY WAY OF POLAND/RUSSIA

SERVES 1
PREP TIME: 5 minutes

2 tablespoons brine from a jar
    of large gherkins (dill pickles)
120 ml (4 fl oz/½ cup) tomato juice
45 ml (1½ fl oz) vodka
¼ teaspoon Worcestershire sauce
¼ teaspoon Tabasco sauce
½ teaspoon grated horseradish
    pinch of freshly ground black
    pepper
1 large gherkin (dill pickle) spear
1 celery stalk, bottom trimmed but
    leaves still intact

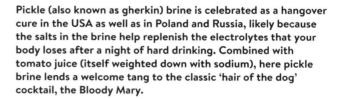

Pickle (also known as gherkin) brine is celebrated as a hangover
cure in the USA as well as in Poland and Russia, likely because
the salts in the brine help replenish the electrolytes that your
body loses after a night of hard drinking. Combined with
tomato juice (itself weighted down with sodium), here pickle
brine lends a welcome tang to the classic 'hair of the dog'
cocktail, the Bloody Mary.

1. In a cocktail shaker, combine the brine with the tomato juice,
    vodka, Worcestershire sauce, Tabasco sauce, horseradish and
    black pepper.
2. Fill the shaker with ice and shake until cold.
3. Place a gherkin spear into a tall glass along with the
    celery stalk.
4. Pour the contents of the shaker along with the ice into the
    glass and serve.

Canadians also relieve hangovers with a variant of the Bloody
Mary called the Bloody Caesar, which puts a spin on the tomato-
vodka classic by adding a lashing of briny clam juice or using
Clamato juice instead of tomato juice. Invented in Calgary by
bartender Walter Chell in 1969, the cocktail has quickly become
the country's most popular mixed drink, with more than
418 million Caesars consumed each year. Pretty impressive for a
country of about 37 million inhabitants, eh?

PICKLEBACK

USA

SERVES 1
PREP TIME: 1 minute

45 ml (1½ fl oz) chilled gherkin
  (dill pickle) brine
45 ml (1½ fl oz) whiskey

For those times when you're simply too knackered to cobble together the Pickle Brine Bloody Mary (page 28), you can't beat the effortlessness of the Pickleback – a shot of whiskey followed by a shot of brine. Jameson Irish whiskey is the preferred brand for this drink – also sometimes referred to as a 'piskey whickle' – but, really, anything that's brown and boozy will do.

1. Pour the brine into a shot glass.
2. Pour the whiskey into a different shot glass.
3. Knock back the whiskey, then chase it with the shot of brine. Repeat as needed.

FERNET CON COCA

ARGENTINA

SERVES 1
PREP TIME: 1 minute

60 ml (2 fl oz) Fernet-Branca
180 ml (6 fl oz) Coca-Cola

Argentina's favourite cocktail (sometimes referred to as a Fernando or a Fernandito) might be the source of many a hangover, but it can also do double-duty as a morning-after remedy, thanks to the bevy of bitter, herbal ingredients (myrrh in particular) in Fernet-Branca said to settle the stomach. Fernet-Branca is actually an Italian *amaro*, or herbal bitter liqueur, most often enjoyed as a digestif after dinner, but following a big marketing push in the 1980s and 1990s, it became Argentina's go-to, anytime drink. In fact, today Argentinians consume more than 75 per cent of the world's market share of the liqueur.

1. Fill a highball glass with ice and top with the Fernet-Branca. Add the Coca-Cola and stir to combine.

CORPSE REVIVER NO. 2

SERVES 1
PREP TIME: 5 minutes

---

30 ml (1 fl oz) gin

30 ml (1 fl oz) Lillet

30 ml (1 fl oz) Cointreau

30 ml (1 fl oz) freshly squeezed
lemon juice

1 teaspoon absinthe or other
anise-flavoured liqueur

orange peel, for garnish

The Corpse Reviver No. 2 is the most popular and enduring of all the drinks found in the family of classic cocktails known as Corpse Revivers, so named for their ability to resuscitate the near-dead after a night of debauchery. Harry Craddock, author of the seminal *Savoy Cocktail Handbook* and bartender at the London hotel's famed American Bar, notes that the Corpse Reviver No. 1 (a potent combo of Cognac, brandy and vermouth) ought to be consumed 'before 11 a.m., or whenever steam and energy are needed'. A double shot of brandy so early in the day, though, may send you right back to bed, so a better bet is the Corpse Reviver No. 2, a light, citrus-spiked tipple. But take heed – Craddock also warns that consuming four Corpse Reviver No. 2s in quick succession will without doubt 'unrevive the corpse again'.

1. Combine the gin, Lillet, Cointreau, lemon juice and absinthe in a cocktail shaker along with a few cubes of ice and shake until well chilled. Pour into a coupe or martini glass and garnish with an orange peel floating on top.

CHAMPAGNE PICK-ME-UP

SERVES 1
PREP TIME: 5 minutes

---

30 ml (1 fl oz) Cognac

1½ teaspoons freshly squeezed orange juice

1 dash grenadine

1 dash Angostura bitters

120 ml (4 fl oz) Champagne or other dry sparkling wine

When you need something bubbly and refreshing with a lilt of sweetness to alleviate a hangover and your trusty Berocca or Alka-Seltzer just won't cut it, look to the aptly named Champagne Pick-Me-Up. A popular libation at Paris's Ritz Bar in the early 20th century, think of this classic cocktail as an upgrade on your brunchtime mimosa.

1. Combine the Cognac, orange juice, grenadine and bitters in a shaker filled with ice. Shake until well chilled and strain into a Champagne flute.
2. Top with the Champagne and serve.

MICHELADA

SERVES 1
PREP TIME: 5 minutes

2 limes, halved
2 tablespoons Tajín seasoning
½ teaspoon Maggi sauce
2 dashes Worcestershire sauce
¾ teaspoon hot sauce,
   preferably Valentina
1 x 330 ml (12-fl oz) bottle
   Pilsner-style lager

Having a beer the morning after
a night of drinking is a common
hangover remedy around the
world, particularly in Western
Europe and Scandinavia. In
Denmark, for instance, it's
known as a *reparationsbajer*
or 'recovery beer' while in
Germany it's called a *konterbier*,
or 'counter beer'.

There are as many recipes for micheladas as there are hungover
hombres in church on a given Sunday morning in Puebla. Yet
most Mexicans agree that this refreshing, lime-kissed beer
cocktail should be served ice cold, and is best enjoyed under the
mid-morning sun. This recipe is entirely adaptable – if you like
a spicier cocktail, add more hot sauce (Valentina is *de rigeur* in
Mexico, but feel free to use whatever's on hand). If you want
more savoury funk, up the Maggi sauce, or even add in a splash
of Clamato (a tomato juice flavoured with clam juice). Tajín is
a Mexican seasoning blend of mild chillies, lime and salt; it's
available online or in Latin supermarkets but, if you can't find it,
substitute 1 teaspoon mild chilli powder combined with
1 tablespoon sea salt flakes.

1. Rub one half of a lime around the rim of a pint glass, then
   juice all of the lime halves – you should end up with around
   3 tablespoons of juice. If there's more than this, discard the
   extra juice or be thrifty and freeze it in an ice cube tray for
   future use.
2. Place the Tajín seasoning on a small plate with a diameter a
   little larger than the pint glass. Dip the moistened part of the
   glass into the seasoning to coat the rim with the spice mix.
3. Pour the lime juice, Maggi sauce, Worcestershire sauce and
   hot sauce into the glass and fill with ice. Top with the beer and
   stir gently to combine.

HANGOVER HELPER

EXTRA GINGERY DARK AND STORMY

SERVES 1
PREP TIME: 5 minutes

---

1 teaspoon finely grated ginger

juice of ½ lime, plus a lime slice, to serve

45 ml (1½ fl oz) rum (ideally Goslings Black Seal Rum)

240 ml (8 fl oz/1 cup) ginger beer

Ginger has long been hailed as a cure for nausea, one of the most commonly cited hangover symptoms. This rendition of the classic Dark 'n Stormy – invented in Bermuda and still treasured there by tourists and locals alike – packs a punch with freshly grated ginger along with the requisite ginger beer. Using a Microplane grater turns the ginger almost paste-like, allowing it to dissolve easily and ensuring you don't end up slurping down any tough, stringy bits. If you don't have one, though, just use your grater's finest hole. Bermuda's own Goslings Black Seal Rum is the gold standard for this drink as it adds a sweet, almost vanilla-like quality to the cocktail. If you can't have a lie down on the beach – an activity pretty much guaranteed to assuage a hangover – this drink makes for a good Plan B.

1. In a tall glass filled with ice, stir together the grated ginger, lime juice and rum.
2. Slowly pour the ginger beer into the glass. Stir briefly to combine and garnish the glass with a lime slice.

EYE OPENER COCKTAIL

SERVES 1
PREP TIME: 5 minutes

45 ml (1½ fl oz) dark rum

15 ml (½ fl oz) Cointreau

15 ml (½ fl oz) Bailey's Irish Cream liqueur

1 dash anise-flavoured liqueur, such as pastis, ouzo or absinthe

1 raw egg yolk

An Eye Opener can refer to any drink to be consumed before the clock strikes noon, though in the cocktail canon, the Eye Opener itself generally refers to a rum-based drink prepared with a raw egg yolk. Full of protein, raw egg yolks are touted as hangover cures around the world (in Hong Kong, for instance, you may find rice topped with Bolognese sauce and a raw egg yolk on top as a purported hangover cure). This cocktail, which I like to think of as a complete breakfast (it marries the flavours of coffee, orange juice and eggs), is a little more palatable than the most common raw egg hangover cure: the Prairie Oyster (page 44).

1. Combine the dark rum, Cointreau, Bailey's Irish Cream, anise-flavoured liqueur and egg yolk in a shaker filled with ice.
2. Shake vigorously until cold, then strain into a martini glass.

PRAIRIE OYSTER

USA

SERVES 1
PREP TIME: 1 minute

1 egg
2 dashes Tabasco sauce
*¼ teaspoon red or white
   wine vinegar*
2 dashes Worcestershire sauce
tiny sprinkle of salt
tiny grinding of black pepper

The precise origin of the Prairie Oyster is hazy, but this hangover remedy – so named because the texture of the raw egg recalls that of a raw oyster – was popularised in New England in the late 19th century. Since then, everyone from *Cabaret*'s Sally Bowles to James Bond has knocked back the concoction, all in the name of curing throbbing heads and nausea. If the thought of consuming a raw egg when hungover is in itself nauseating, I can assure you that it goes down easier than you'd expect.

1. Crack the egg into a rocks glass, making sure to leave the yolk unbroken. If the yolk breaks, throw away or keep in an airtight container to use for another recipe and start with a new egg.
2. Add the Tabasco sauce, vinegar, Worcestershire sauce, salt and pepper to the glass.
3. To drink, knock back in one gulp.

ICED COCONUT MATCHA

JAPAN BY WAY OF THE TROPICS

SERVES 1
PREP TIME: 5 minutes

1 teaspoon matcha powder
240 ml (8 fl oz/1 cup)
    coconut water

Rehydration is essential when dealing with a hangover, and coconut water is an excellent source of electrolytes. It's for this reason that coconut water is often heralded as a hangover remedy in Brazil and the Philippines and other tropical locales. Green tea itself is also a great source of antioxidants, so when you put these two super drinks together, you've got one hell of a backed-by-science hangover cure! Okay, so maybe science hasn't officially endorsed *this* drink, but coconut matcha is definitely thirst-quenching and great tasting. Use a high-quality coconut water, and if you can't find matcha powder at your local shop, it can be bought online or at Asian supermarkets.

1. Combine the matcha powder and 60 ml (2 fl oz/¼ cup) boiling water in a small bowl or mug and whisk until fully combined.
2. Pour the prepared matcha mixture and the coconut water into a shaker filled with ice. Shake vigorously until cold, then pour the contents of the shaker – ice included – into a glass.

TURMERIC LATTE

SERVES 1
PREP TIME: 1 minute
COOK TIME: 10 minutes

½ teaspoon dried turmeric

350 ml (12 fl oz/1½ cups)
   unsweetened light coconut milk

tiny pinch of freshly ground
   black pepper

1 cinnamon stick

2 teaspoons maple syrup

¼ teaspoon vanilla extract

Thought to enhance liver function and aid in digestion, turmeric has long been promoted as a hangover cure in the Far East. In Japan, for instance, you'll find convenience stores stocked with turmeric-based hangover tonics like *Ukon no Chikara*. Likewise, in India, turmeric-based drinks are regularly prepared to cure a bevy of ailments. The West is finally catching on to the magic of turmeric, and no beverage has seen such a rise in popularity from Sydney to San Francisco as the turmeric latte, sometimes referred to as 'golden milk'. This creamy, cosy mug of warmth is a hangover's golden cure, too.

1. Combine all the ingredients in a small saucepan and bring just to a boil, whisking regularly.
2. Remove the pan from the heat and let sit for 5 minutes.
3. Discard the cinnamon stick, whisk vigorously for a few seconds to froth up the latte, pour into a mug and serve immediately.

FLAT 7 UP

SERVES 1
PREP TIME: 1 minute
(Option 1 or 2)
COOK TIME: 1 minute
(Option 2)

---

350 ml (12 fl oz/1½ cups) 7 Up

---

7 Up may be Ireland's magical hangover elixir, but just across the sea in Scotland, Irn-Bru is the hungover lad or lassie's drink of choice. Originally invented at the start of the 20th century and sold under the name 'Iron Brew', the bright orange soft drink has a sweet, almost bubble gum-like flavour and contains 0.002 per cent of ammonium ferric citrate, along with a secret mix of other flavouring agents. When you've had too much of Scotland's national drink, they say there's no better cure than a bottle of Scotland's *other* national drink.

Flat soft drinks have long been offered to unwell children who can't stomach much of anything. The sugars in the soda give a boost of energy and make the drink appealing, while the water helps to hydrate. In Ireland, more so than anywhere else, Flat 7 Up is specifically cherished as a cure-all. In one's youth, it serves to tame coughs, colds, tummy aches and more. In adulthood, well, it's lauded for its ability to cure a hangover. There are two schools of thought on how to serve the soft drink: room temperature and hot. Which one annihilates a hangover better? Only one way to find out – but that's why the weekend has two days!

Option 1: Pour the 7 Up in a glass and stir vigorously with a metal fork for 1 minute to reduce the carbonation in the soda. Alternatively, you can just open a bottle of 7 Up and leave it out for a few days until it's flat, but that takes more advanced preparation, and you never know when a hangover might strike.

Option 2: Pour the 7 Up into a heatproof mug and microwave for 1 minute on high until boiling. Serve immediately.

LEMON-GINGER DETOX

SERVES 1
PREP TIME: 5 minutes

2 tablespoons freshly squeezed lemon juice
2.5 cm (1 in) piece ginger, peeled and thinly sliced
2 tablespoons honey

Ginger is one of the best natural cures for a hangover, helping to settle the stomach and treat everything from inflammation to dizziness. This warming tea pairs the knobby rhizome with honey – another natural powerhouse that's been touted for its medicinal properties throughout the ages. One sip and you'll see why.

1. Combine all ingredients with 375 ml (12½ fl oz/1½ cups) boiling water in a mug.
2. Using a muddler or wooden spoon, lightly crush the ginger to release its flavours. Serve immediately.

LECHE DE TIGRE
TIGER'S MILK

SERVES 1
PREP TIME: 10 minutes
COOK TIME: n/a

*75 g (2½ oz) raw firm white fish,
such as sea bass or pollock,
skin removed and chopped
into chunks*

*50 ml (1¾ fl oz/¼ cup) freshly
squeezed lime juice*

1 tablespoon red onion, chopped

*1 teaspoon chopped coriander
(cilantro)*

*¼ teaspoon finely chopped
habanero or aji amarillo pepper*

¼ teaspoon salt

Leche de Tigre, or 'Tiger's Milk', is the juicy, limey goodness that remains in the bottom of the bowl of *ceviche*, said to be both an aphrodisiac and a hangover cure. That's convenient, since there's rarely a better way of spending a day hungover than in bed with a loved one. You can easily whip up a whole batch of ceviche and wait to slurp up the remains of the milky marinade, but truth be told, a whole bowl of semi-raw fish when you're feeling queasy isn't the most appetising. Fortunately, you can blitz up the components of leche de tigre quickly in a mini food processor; if you don't have one, simply mince and mash up all ingredients until well combined. Be warned, though, that a standard-sized food processor will be too large to accommodate the small amount of ingredients.

1. Place all the ingredients in a mini food processor. Pulse until smooth and combined.
2. Transfer the covered food processor's bowl to the freezer and let chill for 10 minutes. Using a fine mesh sieve (strainer), strain into a shot glass, pressing the mixture to extract the juices, if needed. Discard the solids. Drink immediately.

CHAPTER 2

ALL ABOUT EGGS

Hungover people around the world love eggs, and for good reason: they contain high amounts of cysteine, an amino acid that helps break down the hangover-causing toxin acetaldehyde. Plus, eggs are full of protein, iron and plenty of other vitamins. Not to mention they cook quickly and are delicious to boot. What more could you want?

REVUELTO GRAMAJO
BREAKFAST SCRAMBLE

ARGENTINA

SERVES 2
PREP TIME: 20 minutes
COOK TIME: 15 minutes

---

220 g (8 oz) russet or maris piper potatoes, peeled

3 eggs

1 tablespoon double (heavy) cream

salt and freshly ground black pepper

500 ml (17 fl oz/2 cups) vegetable oil

1 tablespoon butter

60 g (2 oz) onion, chopped

40 g (1⅓ oz) short, thin strips of ham

40 g (1¾ oz) frozen peas

Invented by the rotund Argentinean soldier Artemio Gramajo at the turn of the 20th century, this South American breakfast scramble takes a bit of patience and focus as you have to use a mandoline to cut the potatoes, which are then deep-fried in hot, bubbling oil. If your hands are unsteady from too much Malbec the night before, save this for another day, or omit the potato completely, throw in an extra egg and proceed accordingly to enjoy a nice ham-and-pea scramble. I won't tell Artemio.

1. Use a mandoline or food processor to cut the potatoes into matchstick-sized pieces. Soak the potatoes in a bowl of cold water.

2. Whisk the eggs with the cream in a bowl along with a pinch each of salt and pepper. Set aside.

3. Remove the potatoes from the water and pat dry on paper towels. In a large, heavy-bottomed saucepan, heat the oil to 190°C (375°F). Carefully add the potatoes and deep-fry until golden, about 6½ minutes. Using a slotted spoon, remove the potatoes from the oil and let drain on a paper towel.

4. Melt the butter over medium-high heat in a non-stick frying pan. Add the onion and cook until translucent but not browned, about 2 minutes. Add the ham and peas and cook for another 2 minutes, or until the ham is just starting to brown. Add the fried potatoes to the frying pan and stir to combine. Turn up the heat to high and add the eggs, stirring the mixture constantly until the eggs cook through, about 1 minute or less. Season with black pepper, then transfer to plates and serve.

FULL ENGLISH BREAKFAST

ENGLAND, UK

SERVES 2
PREP TIME: 5 minutes
COOK TIME: 30 minutes

1 small tomato, halved

6 chestnut (cremini) mushrooms, quartered

3 tablespoons butter, melted

¼ teaspoon dried thyme

¼ teaspoon salt

¼ teaspoon freshly ground black pepper

2 slices white sandwich bread, cut in half on the diagonal

½ x 400 g (14 oz) tin baked beans in tomato sauce (preferably Heinz)

4 small pork sausages, such as chipolatas

1 tablespoon vegetable oil

4 slices back bacon

2 eggs

According to the English Breakfast Society (yes, such a thing exists), the traditional full English breakfast dates all the way back to the 1300s. The gentry served the meal in their country estates as a means of displaying their wealth with the variety of meats on offer. The Victorian elite then carried on the tradition and the Edwardians ultimately codified the meal to what it looks like today. There's endless debate about what must or must not be included in a proper fry-up (many will quibble here about the lack of black pudding, no doubt), but everyone agrees that the meal must include, at the very least, eggs, sausages, bacon, baked beans and tomato. And, of course, that it must be accompanied by a proper cup of hot, milky tea.

1. Preheat the oven to 220°C (425°F/Gas 8). In a large bowl, toss the tomato halves and quartered mushrooms with 2 tablespoons of the melted butter, thyme, salt and pepper. Drizzle the remaining tablespoon of butter on the four triangles of bread.
2. Transfer the bread, mushrooms and tomato to a foil-lined baking (cookie) sheet and roast in the oven, turning the items halfway through, until the bread is toasted and golden brown, the mushrooms are golden brown and the tomato has softened and browned. This should take about 7 minutes total for the toast – so remove it from the tray at this point – and 15 minutes total for the tomato and mushrooms. Once cooked, keep warm.

If you've had your fill of the classic English breakfast, look a little further afield and try these regional variations:

IRISH

Swap out the baked beans for a slice each of black pudding and white pudding and swap the toast for Irish soda bread.

SCOTTISH

Swap out the baked beans for a slice of black pudding and a slice of haggis, swap out the toast for tattie scones and use Lorne sausages for the sausage.

ULSTER FRY

Swap out the toast for soda farl and the baked beans for boxty and add a slice of black pudding.

WELSH

Swap out the toast for laverbread and swap out the baked beans for a handful of cockles, fried with the bacon and sausage.

3. While the vegetables are roasting, pour the baked beans (save the remainder of the tin for another day's fry-up) into a small saucepan and bring just to a boil. Stir, then lower the heat to a gentle simmer, keeping on the heat until ready to serve.

4. Fill a non-stick frying pan with 240 ml (8 fl oz/1 cup) water and bring to a boil. Add the sausages and cook for 2 minutes to par-boil them (you'll finish frying them later, so don't worry if they still look semi-raw). Remove the sausages and let dry on a paper towel. Discard the water and wipe the pan dry.

5. Add the oil to the frying pan and turn the heat to medium-high. Add the sausages and bacon and cook, flipping occasionally, until browned, about 5 minutes. Remove the meat from the pan, leaving the fat in the frying pan. Set the meat aside with the vegetables and keep warm.

6. Crack the eggs into the pan and cook sunny-side up so that the whites are firm but the yolks are still runny, about 2 minutes.

7. To assemble, spoon the beans either into two ramekins (if you don't want the bean juices running all over the plate) or spoon into the middle of two plates. Place an egg, 2 sausages, 2 pieces of bacon, a tomato half and a spoonful of mushrooms on each plate surrounding the beans, with the toast on the side. Serve immediately.

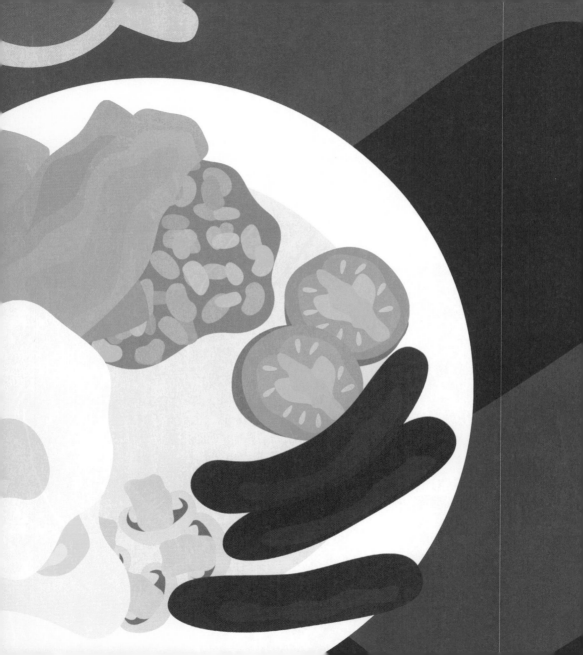

EASY CHILAQUILES

MEXICO

SERVES 2
PREP TIME: 5 minutes
COOK TIME: 10 minutes

¼ red onion, peeled and sliced as
   thinly as possible (using
   a mandoline will help here)

60 ml (2 fl oz/¼ cup) apple cider
   vinegar or red wine vinegar

½ teaspoon salt

1 tablespoon vegetable oil

2 eggs

200 g (7 oz) tortilla crisps (chips),
   preferably ones that are extra
   thick and crunchy

400 ml (13 fl oz/generous
   1½ cups) shop-bought tomatillo
   salsa (also known as salsa verde
   or green salsa)

60 g (2 oz/¼ cup) Mexican crema
   or sour cream thinned with a
   splash of milk

2 heaped tablespoons crumbled
   cotija (ricotta salata or feta, if
   unavailable)

2 tablespoons coriander
   (cilantro) leaves

The genius of Easy Chilaquiles is that it makes eating half a bag
of tortilla chips and salsa a socially acceptable breakfast. Far and
away one of my favourite things to eat hungover, chilaquiles are
a Mexican staple of crisp-soft tortilla crisps (chips) swimming in
salsa. I'm partial to *salsa verde*, made with tangy tomatillos but,
by all means, feel free to swap it out for your preferred tomato-
based red salsa.

1. First, prepare the pickled onions: place the red onion slices,
   vinegar and salt in a small bowl and let sit while you prepare
   the remaining ingredients.
2. Heat the oil in a non-stick frying pan over medium-high heat.
   Crack the eggs into the frying pan and cook sunny-side up
   until the whites are firm but the yolks are still runny, about
   2 minutes. Remove the eggs from the pan and set aside.
3. Return the frying pan to the heat and add the tortilla crisps
   and tomatillo salsa. Cook, stirring occasionally, until the crisps
   have softened but are not mushy, about 3 minutes.
4. Divide the crisps between two bowls and top each with
   an egg. Drizzle each bowl with the crema and top with the
   cheese and coriander. Remove the pickled onions from the
   pickling liquid and scatter on top.

KAYA TOAST WITH HALF-BOILED EGGS

SERVES 2
PREP TIME: 5 minutes
COOK TIME: 10 minutes

4 slices soft white sandwich
  bread, crusts removed

4 tablespoons kaya (coconut jam)

2 tablespoons cold salted butter,
  thinly sliced

4 eggs

1 teaspoon dark (or regular)
  soy sauce

pinch of white pepper

Singapore might not stand out as one of the world's big drinking meccas, but it does know its way around a hangover breakfast. The Southeast Asian city-state's favourite treat come daybreak is Kaya Toast, a simple sandwich of salted butter and rich, eggy coconut jam, accompanied by two barely cooked eggs for dunking. It's the perfect marriage of textures and flavours, with the soft, salty, soy-dressed eggs, the sweet, creamy kaya and the crunchy toast. The Hainanese brought the dish to Singapore and now it's found all over the island (and Malaysia, too), from popular chains to tiny family-run hawker stalls.

1. Toast the bread in a toaster or under the grill (broiler) so that both sides are golden brown. Spread 1 tablespoon of kaya on each of the slices of bread, then top two of the slices with the cold salted butter. Place the unbuttered slice, kaya-side down, on top of the buttered slice to make a sandwich. Cut each sandwich in half lengthways and set aside.

2. Bring a small saucepan of water to a boil. Lower the heat to a simmer, then gently crack the eggs into the pan and cook, covered, for 2 minutes. Carefully (use a combination of a slotted spoon and pouring the water out from the pan) transfer two eggs apiece in a small bowl or ramekin. The eggs should be jiggly and look barely cooked; they act almost as a sauce in this dish rather than being a poached egg accompaniment.

3. To serve, sprinkle the soy sauce and white pepper over the two bowls of eggs. Dip the kaya toast into the runny eggs for a perfect bite.

LOCO MOCO

SERVES 2
PREP TIME: 5 minutes
(assuming you've got cooked rice in your refrigerator)
COOK TIME: 25 minutes

150 g (5 oz) beef mince
   (ground beef)
50 g (2 oz) onion, finely grated
2 teaspoons panko breadcrumbs
¼ teaspoon salt
large pinch of freshly
   ground pepper
2 tablespoons cold butter
1 teaspoon cornflour (cornstarch)
120 ml (4 fl oz/½ cup) beef stock
½ teaspoon soy sauce
1 teaspoon oyster sauce
2 eggs
180 g (6½ oz/1 cup) hot cooked
   white rice

It might sound pretty *loco* to start off the day with a large plate of rice topped with a hamburger and a fried egg, all drowning in beef gravy. Yet Loco Moco is a Hawaiian brunch staple that was invented (with the help of some hungry teenagers) in 1949 at the Lincoln Grill in Hilo on the Big Island. It's comfort food that truly captures the *aloha* spirit and Hawaii's 'plate lunch' culture.

1. Combine the beef, half of the grated onion, the panko breadcrumbs and the salt and pepper in a large bowl, mixing until combined, but taking care not to overmix. Shape into two flat patties.
2. Melt ½ tablespoon butter in a frying pan over medium-high heat. Add the patties and let cook, untouched, for about 4 minutes. When nicely browned, flip over and cook on the other side for another 4 minutes. Remove the patties and set aside.
3. Add the remaining grated onion to the pan. Stir with a wooden spoon, scraping up the browned bits of meat stuck to the frying pan. When the onion turns translucent, about 30 seconds later, stir in the cornflour. Cook for another 30 seconds before adding the beef stock, soy sauce and oyster sauce. Turn the heat up to high and cook until thick and gravy-like, about 3 minutes. Stir in 1 tablespoon of the butter.
4. Meanwhile, heat the remaining butter in a non-stick frying pan. Crack in the eggs and cook sunny-side up so that the whites are firm but the yolks are runny, about 2 minutes.
5. To serve, place a mound of hot rice on a plate. Top with the hamburger patty and egg and spoon a generous amount of gravy over the top.

SHAKSHUKA

SERVES 2
PREP TIME: 10 minutes
COOK TIME: 30 minutes

2 tablespoons olive oil

¼ red onion, thinly sliced

½ red (bell) pepper, thinly sliced

½ teaspoon ground cumin

¼ teaspoon smoked paprika

¼ teaspoon salt

1 tablespoon harissa paste

400 g (14 oz) tin chopped
   tomatoes

4 eggs

50 g (2 oz/⅓ cup) crumbled feta

1 tablespoon finely chopped
   coriander (cilantro)

Shakshuka's had a bit of a golden moment in recent years, popping up at trendy brunch spots and on Instagram alike. The dish, which consists of eggs poached in a spicy tomato sauce, hails from Northern Africa, but is most relished as breakfast – that's to say, hangover food – in Israel. Use a smaller frying pan for this dish so the liquid doesn't evaporate as quickly; a 20 cm (8 in) pan should do the trick. And make sure to have plenty of crusty bread or toasted pitta on hand to sop up all the extra sauce.

1. Heat the olive oil in a 20 cm (8 in) frying pan over medium-high heat. Add the onion, pepper, cumin, smoked paprika and salt. Cook until the vegetables have softened, about 5 minutes.
2. Add the harissa and tomatoes. Once the sauce reaches a boil, turn the heat to low and cook, covered, for 15 minutes, until a little thickened. Taste and season with more salt, if necessary.
3. Using a spoon, hollow out four depressions in the sauce and crack an egg into each one. Cover and continue cooking until the whites are firm, about 7 minutes.
4. Ladle the eggs and sauce into the two bowls and top with the feta and coriander.

If you're searching for an egg dish that goes beyond the standard fried-scrambled-poached offerings, a bowl of *changua* might be the hangover food you've been craving. Hailing from Colombia, the popular (if polarising) egg drop soup features a milk-based broth and is served with a *calado*, a piece of dried out, crusty bread, which softens in the coriander-flecked liquid.

CHAPTER 3

MAIN DISH CARBS

Sometimes you just need a lot of carby, starchy food when you're hungover. Dishes that gloss your lips with oil and fill your stomach. It's all here: potatoes, noodles, bread, rice and everything nice.

GINGER AND SPRING ONION CONGEE

CHINA

SERVES 2
PREP TIME: 5 minutes
COOK TIME: 1¾ hours

100 g (3½ oz/½ cup) short or medium-grain white rice

1 litre (34 fl oz/4 cups) water

500 ml (17½ fl oz/2 cups) chicken stock

½ teaspoon salt

2.5 cm (1 in) piece ginger, peeled and cut into thin strips

3 large spring onions (scallions) white and light green parts only, thinly sliced

soy sauce, to serve

monosodium glutamate powder (MSG), to serve

Congee, a rice-based gruel popular for breakfast throughout China, has little-to-no taste or texture on its own, making it an ideal first food for babies. It is also hangover fare par excellence. I top off this ginger-spring onion congee with a sprinkling of soy sauce and a dash of MSG – on that note, do not fear MSG! It's a commonly used salt that boosts the flavour of whatever you're cooking, and many studies have shown that it's perfectly safe. Feel free to jazz up the bowl with whatever strikes your fancy: poached shredded chicken or prawns (shrimp) would be lovely, or you could add a handful of fried shallots, crushed peanuts, sesame oil, pickled vegetables, chilli sauce, meatballs, hard-boiled eggs – you've got carte blanche when it comes to crowning your congee.

1. Place the rice, water, chicken stock and salt into a large saucepan and bring to a boil over high heat. Stirring occasionally, turn the heat to low and cook, partially covered, for about 1¼ –1½ hours, or until the rice is completely soft and breaking down and the soup has a porridge-like consistency. If the mixture looks too runny, continue cooking for longer. If it looks too dry, add a little more water to the pan.
2. Stir in the ginger and spring onions and cook for another 2 minutes. Ladle into two soup bowls and season to taste with soy sauce and/or MSG, if desired, or any other condiments you'd like to add.

KIMCHI BACON FRIED RICE

SOUTH KOREA MEETS USA

SERVES 2, generously
PREP TIME: 10 minutes
COOK TIME: 15 minutes

2 garlic cloves, finely minced

1 tablespoon soy sauce

1 teaspoon sesame oil

1 tablespoon gochujang
 (Korean chilli paste)

3 eggs

pinch of salt

1 tablespoon vegetable oil

4 strips streaky bacon, chopped

½ large onion, finely diced

275 g (10 oz/2 cups) cold,
 cooked, day-old rice

300 g (10½ oz) kimchi, roughly
 chopped

Whenever I'm getting takeaway for dinner, I'll order an extra portion or two of plain rice just so I can make fried rice the next morning. Slightly dried-out rice straight from the refrigerator is actually much easier to work with than hot cooked rice, which will stick to the wok and clump together. Even rice that's a few days old is fine to use in this recipe, which is perfect as hangovers always strike when least expected. The other important thing to note when making fried rice is that you want to have all your ingredients prepped and ready to go since everything cooks quickly in the hot wok. Don't be tempted to lower the heat when cooking, either; stirring constantly with a wooden spoon ensures you won't end up with any burnt bits.

Looking for more rice-based hangover dishes? Thais often eat a thick rice porridge called *jok* for breakfast, but they consider *khao tom*, or boiled rice soup, the superior choice. Accented with lemongrass and galangal, khao tom is thinner and less mushy than congee or jok as the grains of rice float in the broth.

1. First, make the sauce: combine the garlic, soy sauce, sesame oil and gochujang in a bowl and whisk to combine. Set aside.
2. Whisk the eggs along with a pinch of salt in a small bowl.
3. Heat the oil in a wok over high heat. Add the eggs and let cook for several seconds, allowing them to puff up around the edge of the wok. Stir occasionally until fully cooked but not browned, about 1 minute. Transfer the eggs to a plate and set aside.
4. Remove the wok from the heat and wipe it out with a paper towel, removing any stuck-on particles of egg. Return the wok to the heat, add the bacon and cook over high heat, stirring constantly. When the bacon is cooked and just beginning to brown, about 2 minutes, use a slotted spoon to remove the bacon, leaving the fat in the wok. Set the cooked bacon aside with the eggs.
5. Add the onion to the wok and cook until translucent, about 1–2 minutes, stirring constantly. Add the rice and stir to combine. Cook for another minute until the rice begins to smell fragrant. Add the kimchi and the soy-gochujang sauce. Stir constantly until the rice is fully coated with the sauce and everything is well combined.
6. Return the eggs and bacon to the pan, breaking up any large pieces of egg with the back of the spoon. Stir until incorporated and serve immediately.

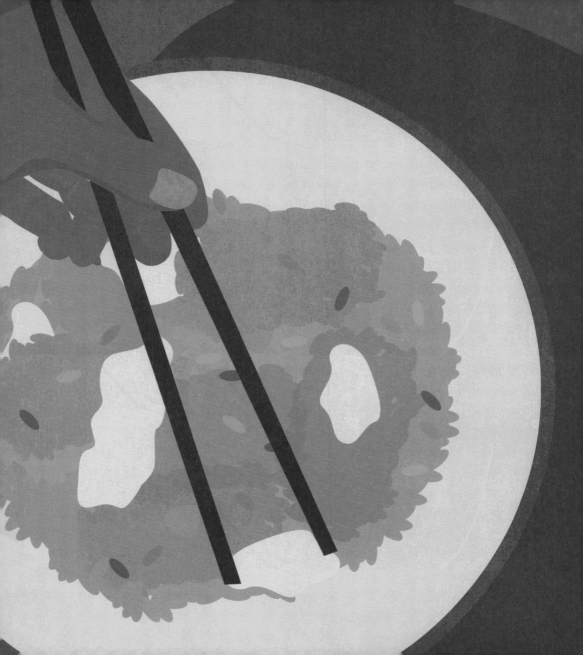

MIDNIGHT SPAGHETTI

ITALY

SERVES 2
PREP TIME: 5 minutes
COOK TIME: 25 minutes

---

250 g (9 oz) spaghetti

60 ml (2 fl oz/¼ cup) olive oil

3 garlic cloves, sliced as thinly as possible

½ teaspoon chilli flakes

1 generous teaspoon chopped parsley

salt

Italy doesn't wait until morning to cure its hangovers. Instead, in the wee hours of the night, at the tail end of a party, Italian revellers will throw together a Spaghettata di Mezzanotte, also known as a midnight spaghetti party, believing the carbs from the pasta will help absorb the excess alcohol in the body. The classic *aglio, olio e peperoncino* (garlic, olive oil and chilli) is a favourite for midnight spaghetti because it takes very little time to prepare and only uses pantry staples.

1. Bring a large saucepan of heavily salted water to a rolling boil. Add the spaghetti to the pan and cook according to the instructions on the packet.
2. When the spaghetti has about 3 minutes' cooking time left, place the olive oil, garlic and chilli flakes in a frying pan large enough to hold all of the spaghetti. Cook over medium heat, stirring regularly, until the garlic has softened and is just slightly golden in colour. The garlic will cook quickly, so watch it to make sure it does not brown or, worse, burn. Remove the pan from the heat if your garlic is beginning to colour but your spaghetti isn't done yet.
3. When the spaghetti is al dente – you still want a noticeable bite to the pasta – reserve 60 ml (2 fl oz/¼ cup) of the cooking water and then drain the pasta.
4. Add the spaghetti and the reserved cooking water to the frying pan. Turn the heat up to high and cook, using tongs to swirl the pasta around the pan, until all of the water is absorbed. Add the parsley and season to taste with salt, stirring to make sure the pasta is completely covered in sauce. Serve immediately.

POUTINE

SERVES 2
PREP TIME: 5 minutes
(A Little Challenging method) or
10 minutes (Difficult method)
COOK TIME: 30 minutes or
(A Little Challenging method) or
40 minutes (Difficult method)

If making French fries from scratch

2 russet or maris piper
   potatoes, peeled

1 litre (34 fl oz/4 cups) vegetable oil

1 teaspoon fine sea salt

If using frozen French fries

1 x 425 g (15 oz) bag frozen
   French fries

For the gravy and cheese

2 tablespoons butter

2 tablespoons plain
   (all-purpose) flour

60 ml (2 fl oz) light lager

120 ml (4 fl oz/½ cup) good-
   quality beef stock

120 ml (4 fl oz/½ cup) good-
   quality chicken stock

continued on next page

How do you exalt one of the world's best hangover foods –
French fries – to even greater culinary heights? Top 'em with
fresh cheese and a rich gravy, that's how. Poutine, a Québécois
staple, does just this, and is the perfect way to eat your feelings
following a long night of drinking. Using pre-cut frozen
French fries will speed this dish along in no time, but the cold
oil technique for cooking French fries is actually very user-
friendly as it requires barely any active time beyond cutting the
potatoes. Ask your local cheesemonger for cheese curds – you
want fresh curds that squeak between your teeth when you bite
into them. If you can't get hold of them, bite-sized pieces of
really good mozzarella will work well in their place.

**Start at step 1 if making the fries from scratch or begin
with step 5 if using frozen ones.**

1. Preheat the oven to 90°C (200°F/Gas ¼).
2. Line a large mixing bowl with a paper towel. Slice the potatoes
   lengthways into 1 cm (⅓ in) thick slices. Lay the slices flat and
   cut 1 cm (⅓ in) wide batons so that the potatoes are now
   shaped like French fries. Transfer the potatoes to a large,
   heavy-bottomed saucepan and cover completely with the oil.
3. Turn the heat to high and cook until the oil is rapidly boiling,
   about 5 minutes. Lower the heat to medium-high and
   continue frying until the potatoes are golden brown. This
   may take anywhere from 12–25 minutes, depending on
   the heat of your burners. You want to let the fries cook
   uninterrupted for the first 10 minutes or so, but then you
   can turn the fries occasionally with tongs or a slotted spoon
   to check their progress.

1 teaspoon ketchup

salt and freshly ground
   black pepper

90 g (3 oz) fresh cheese curds
   or very good-quality mozzarella,
   at room temperature, and cut
   into bite-sized pieces if large

4. Quickly remove the fries from the oil and transfer to the mixing bowl lined with a paper towel. Sprinkle the fries with salt and toss in the bowl until coated. Transfer to a roasting tin or baking (cookie) sheet and keep warm in the oven until ready to serve.

5. If using frozen French fries, cook them according to the instructions on the packet.

6. To make the gravy, melt the butter in a saucepan over high heat and add the flour. Stir constantly (it may look dry and clumpy) until dark golden in colour, about 2 minutes.

7. Slowly add in the lager, beef stock, chicken stock, ketchup, and a pinch of salt and pepper, whisking until smooth. Bring to a boil and cook at high heat for about 5 minutes, or until thickened.

8. To serve, divide the French fries between two plates. Top with the cheese curds and pour the piping hot gravy over the top so as to slightly melt the cheese curds. Serve immediately.

PEPPERONI PIZZA BAGEL

USA

SERVES 1 as a filling meal
or 2 as a snack
PREP TIME: 5 minutes
COOK TIME: 15 minutes

---

1 plain (or wholewheat,
   if you're feeling virtuous) bagel,
   sliced in half lengthwise

4 tablespoons jarred pizza sauce
   or tomato sauce

2 teaspoons grated Pecorino
   Romano

80 g (3 oz) grated low-moisture
   mozzarella

large pinch of chilli flakes

10 pepperoni slices

2 teaspoons finely chopped basil

Oh, the pizza bagel, the lovechild of two of the greatest breads ever created. While the true origins are murky (some say the pizza bagel was created at a bagel shop in Woodland Hills, California, in 1974), many Americans have a childhood association with the Ore-Ida frozen Bagel Bites, whose catchy jingle went, 'Pizza in the morning. Pizza in the evening. Pizza at suppertime. When pizza's on a bagel, you can eat pizza anytime'. Beyond being a school day's snack, the pizza bagel has found new life as a hangover treat, ticking off all the major food groups: carbs, salt, meat, fat. This version ups the gourmet factor yet is almost as easy as zapping a frozen bagel in the microwave.

1. Preheat the oven to 200°C (400°F/Gas 6). Place the bagel halves, cut-side up, on a foil-lined baking (cookie) sheet. Bake for 5 minutes until the edges of the bagel are just beginning to turn golden.
2. Remove the bagel from the oven. Divide the tomato sauce between the bagel halves, spreading it evenly. Sprinkle the Pecorino on top of the sauce, followed by the mozzarella and chilli flakes. Finally, top with the pepperoni.
3. Return the baking sheet to the oven and bake the pizza bagels for about 6 minutes, or until the cheese is fully melted and the pepperoni edges are starting to crisp and curl up.
4. Remove from the oven and sprinkle with the basil. Serve immediately.

CRÊPES WITH NUTELLA & BANANAS

FRANCE

SERVES 2 (makes about 6 crêpes)
PREP TIME: 10 minutes
COOK TIME: 15 minutes

---

65 g (2½ oz/1 cup) plain (all-purpose) flour

240 ml (8 fl oz/1 cup) full-fat (whole) milk

1 egg

2 tablespoons melted butter

pinch of salt

2 tablespoons caster (granulated) sugar

¼ teaspoon vanilla extract

2 teaspoons vegetable oil

1–2 bananas, thinly sliced

6 tablespoons Nutella

Ask a Frenchman what he eats when he's hungover and he'll reply that he doesn't get hungover because, *bien sûr*, French people don't drink to excess. That's a lie. French people most certainly do get hangovers. And while flaky croissants and buttered baguettes from the local bakery might take centre stage on a Parisian's breakfast table, the truth is nothing soothes a hangover better than crêpes. Specifically, crêpes with Nutella and sliced bananas. Cooking and flipping crêpes takes some practise (check out a YouTube tutorial if the closest Frenchman is too hungover to demonstrate), but the batter comes together quickly and can even be made the night before and left in the refrigerator, so all you have to do is pour it into a hot pan come morning.

1. Combine the flour, milk, egg, melted butter, salt, sugar and vanilla in a mixing bowl (preferably one with a pour spout) and whisk well until combined.
2. Pour the vegetable oil into a non-stick frying pan, then use a paper towel to wipe the oil all around the pan, sopping up any excess oil. You want the pan to be well-oiled but without any visible pools of oil.

If you're not a fan of Nutella (though is that even possible?), these other classic French fillings will delight instead:

Sweet:
- Melted butter and sugar
- A good berry jam
- Apple compote
- Dark chocolate sauce
- Chestnut cream
- Lemon juice and icing (confectioner's) sugar

Savoury (omit the sugar and vanilla from the crepe batter):
- A fried egg
- Grated Gruyère and ham
- Goat's cheese and tomato
- Tuna, a fried egg and grated Gruyère
- Grated Gruyère, diced roast chicken and fried mushrooms

3. Turn the heat to medium-high. When the frying pan is hot, pour enough batter (about 50 ml/1¾ fl oz/3 tablespoons) into the frying pan, lifting it and rotating it around so the batter runs into a very thin, even layer. If you've put too much batter in the pan, tip any excess back into the batter bowl (the crêpe may look a little wonky but will still taste good).

4. After about 45 seconds, gently lift the crêpe to see if the underside is golden brown. If not, continue cooking until it is. Once golden brown, gently lift the crêpe using a small, thin spatula and flip over. If the pan seems like it is getting too hot, lower the heat. While the other side is cooking, spread 1 tablespoon of Nutella all over the top of the crêpe (it'll melt while you do this, making it easier to spread). Place a few slices of banana on one half of the crêpe.

5. Once the bottom side of the crêpe is fully cooked, fold the crêpe in half so it looks like a half moon stuffed with bananas. Then fold that half in half so it now looks triangular shaped. Transfer to a plate.

6. Without adding more oil to the frying pan, repeat the process until all the crêpes are cooked, stuffed and folded, adjusting the heat as needed. Serve immediately.

MINCE AND CHEESE PIE

NEW ZEALAND

SERVES 8
PREP TIME: 15 minutes
COOK TIME: 2½ hours
(includes baking and
chilling times)

---

2 tablespoons butter, plus extra
    for greasing
1 small carrot, finely chopped
1 celery stalk, finely chopped
1 very small onion, finely chopped
2 garlic cloves, finely chopped
500 g (1 lb 2 oz) beef mince
    (ground beef)
2 tablespoons plain
    (all-purpose) flour
1 tablespoon Worcestershire sauce
½ teaspoon Dijon mustard
½ teaspoon salt
¼ teaspoon freshly ground
    black pepper
240 ml (8 fl oz/1 cup) beef stock
400 g (14 oz) all-butter puff pastry
100 g (3½ oz) mature
    Cheddar, grated
1 egg, beaten

Whether procured from a swank café on an Auckland high street
or from the to-go counter at the local petrol station, there's
no food that powers New Zealand (and, specifically, hungover
Kiwis) more than the mince and cheese pie. Much like the
British sausage roll (page 160), flaky, meaty mince and cheese
pies are often eaten on the go. This version feeds a crowd and
also makes for a wonderful weekend supper when accompanied
by a green salad. The recipe takes a bit of advance planning, but
shop-bought puff pastry helps shorten the cooking process (be
sure to thaw it in advance if using frozen), and you can easily
prep all the vegetables by chucking them in a food processor
and blitzing until finely chopped.

1. Heat the butter in a large saucepan over medium-high heat.
   When the butter begins to foam, add the carrot, celery, onion
   and garlic and cook until softened, about 5 minutes.
2. Add the beef and continue cooking, breaking up any
   large chunks with a wooden spoon, until the meat is no longer
   pink and raw-looking, about 3 minutes. Add the flour and
   stir until fully incorporated. Add the Worcestershire sauce,
   mustard, salt, pepper and beef stock and bring to a boil. Once
   boiling, lower the heat to a simmer and cook, uncovered, for
   15 minutes.
3. Transfer the beef mince to a bowl and chill until completely
   cold, about an hour. Sticking it in the freezer will speed up the
   process to about 30 minutes, but don't forget about it and
   end up with a giant beefy ice cube!

4. Preheat the oven to 200°C (400°F/Gas 6). On a sheet of baking parchment, roll out two-thirds of the puff pastry into a large circle to form the pie's crust. Roll the remaining third of the puff pastry into a smaller circle to form the top of the pie.

5. Lightly grease a deep pie dish with the remaining butter and use the larger pastry disc to line it – the dough should just hang over the top of the top of the dish. Spoon the chilled mince filling into it, scatter over the cheese, then top with the smaller pastry disc. Fold the overhanging pastry from the bottom disc over the top of the smaller disc and then crimp the edges so that the filling is completely encased. Using a sharp knife, make four small slits in the middle of the pie to allow steam to escape. Brush the pastry with the beaten egg.

6. Bake the pie until dark golden brown, about 35 minutes. Remove from the oven and let cool. If it seems like there is a little excess fat from the filling pooling in the tin when you remove it from the oven, carefully tip the pie tin sideways to pour it away. When the pie is cool enough to handle, remove it from the pie tin and transfer it to a cooling rack (using two flat spatulas should do the trick). Serve hot, warm or at room temperature.

PAD KEE MAO
DRUNKEN NOODLES

SERVES 2
PREP TIME: 15 minutes
COOK TIME: 10 minutes

1 tablespoon oyster sauce

2 teaspoons brown sugar

1 tablespoon fish sauce

1 teaspoon soy sauce

3 Thai chillies, such as bird's eye, chopped

2 garlic cloves

2 tablespoons vegetable oil

3 small shallots, quartered lengthways

½ red (bell) pepper, thinly sliced

4 pieces Chinese broccoli (kai lan) or kale, leaves only, roughly chopped

100 g (3½ oz/¾ cup) cherry tomatoes, halved

320 g (11 oz) fresh flat rice noodles

1 handful Thai basil or holy basil

Much like Italy's midnight spaghetti, Thailand's *pad kee mao* is a spicy noodle stir-fry often enjoyed while out on the town. That said, the dish, whose name literally translates to 'fried drunkard', has also become a favourite of hungover students around the world craving the magical restorative power of sweet-but-spicy noodles. Fresh rice noodles can be found at pretty much every Asian supermarket; if you can't find them, substitute dried rice noodles cooked according to the instructions on the packet.

1. Combine the oyster sauce, brown sugar, fish sauce and soy sauce in a small bowl and set aside.
2. Place the chillies in a mortar with the garlic and pound them with the pestle until paste-like.
3. Heat the vegetable oil in a wok over high heat. Add the garlic and chilli paste, stir quickly and then immediately add the shallots and pepper and cook, stirring constantly, until the shallots are beginning to soften, about a minute or so. Add the Chinese broccoli leaves and cherry tomatoes and cook for another 2 minutes, stirring constantly.
4. Add the rice noodles and sauce mixture and stir-fry, stirring until combined. When almost all of the sauce has been absorbed, add in the Thai basil and continue stir-frying until wilted.
5. Divide the noodles between two plates and serve immediately.

CHAPTER 4

SAVOURY SOUPS AND STEWS

Hangover soups and stews weave a common thread among the tapestry of global hangover cuisine. Seemingly every country in South America, Eastern Europe and Asia has its own rendition of a 'hangover soup'. Some are light broths while others are rich, decadent stews. Yet no matter what the ingredients are, they all add up to a bowl of comfort.

KONGNAMUL GUKBAP
JEONJU-STYLE HANGOVER SOUP

SOUTH KOREA

SERVES 2
PREP TIME: 20 minutes
(assuming you've already got
cooked rice in the refrigerator)
COOK TIME: 45 minutes

For the broth

15 g (½ oz) large dried anchovies
  (about 13 pieces)
10 cm (4 in) piece dried kelp

For the soup

175 g (6 oz) beansprouts

3 garlic cloves, finely minced

3 spring onions (scallions),
  thinly sliced

20 g (¾ oz) Korean green chillies,
  very thinly sliced (substitute
  jalapeño if not available,
  adjusting for taste; the peppers
  should provide a hint of heat
  but not be overly spicy)

½ teaspoon salt

2 eggs

185 g (6½ oz/1 cup) piping hot
  cooked short-grain rice

continued on next page

South Korea has a robust drinking culture – not to mention
an equally strong anti-hangover drinks industry that grosses
around £127 million ($165 million) each year. Grab-and-go
bottled drinks may have the convenience factor the morning
after a rough night, but a decidedly more delicious hangover
remedy is *haejangguk*, otherwise known as 'hangover soup'.
Haejangguk actually refers to a given category of soups, with each
region of South Korea having its own speciality. The recipe below,
kongnamul gukbap, is prepared with beansprouts, which are rich
in the amino acid asparagine, said to help the liver break down
acetaldehyde, that compound known to contribute to hangovers.
The soup is traditionally served in a large, individual bowl called
a *ttukbaegi*, which you can place directly over a heat source. In
some restaurants, the egg is served in the soup, while in others,
it's served separately in a small bowl along with the seaweed. I've
modified the soup here to be prepared for two in a large saucepan
and then ladled into bowls for serving at the table.

1. First, make the broth: snap off and discard the heads
    of the anchovies, then dig out and discard the black intestines
    from the middle of the bodies. Place the cleaned anchovies,
    kelp and 1 litre (34 fl oz/4 cups) water in a large stockpot and
    bring to a boil over high heat. Once the broth comes to a boil,
    cover and then lower the heat to a simmer for 30 minutes.
2. Meanwhile, rinse the beansprouts under cold water and
    discard any sprouts that are wilting or discoloured. Prepare all
    the garnishes if you haven't already.

HANGOVER HELPER

For the garnish

2 teaspoons toasted sesame
seeds, partially ground in
a pestle and mortar

¼ teaspoon Korean or other spicy
chilli powder

1 spring onion (scallion), green
parts only, thinly sliced

1 teaspoon crumbled seaweed
sheets (known as gim in Korea
or nori in Japan)

½ teaspoon Korean salted prawns
(shrimp), (optional; or use salt
to taste)

75 g (2½ oz) kimchi,
to serve

3. Once the broth is done, use a slotted spoon to remove and discard the solids. Return the heat to high, and when the broth is boiling, add the beansprouts, garlic, spring onion, chillies and salt, stirring to combine. Cook at a boil, covered, for 5 minutes.
4. Lower the heat to a simmer, then gently crack an egg into a ladle and lower it into the stockpot. Repeat with the other egg. Cover and continue cooking for another 1–2 minutes until the whites firm up slightly but the yolks are still runny.
5. Divide the hot rice into two serving bowls. Ladle the beansprout soup into each bowl, covering the rice and being careful not to break the egg yolk.
6. Top each bowl with all of the garnishes, apart from the kimchi. Serve immediately with a small bowl of kimchi on the side.

Ready to explore more types of Korean hangover soups? In Seoul and its surrounding areas, you're likely to find *Yangpyeong haejangguk*, which features coagulated ox blood in a savoury, beefy soya bean paste broth along with a bevy of vegetables. In the Gangwon province, on the other hand, you're more likely to find a hangover soup called *hwangtae haejangguk*, prepared with dried pollock. In Busan, pork and rice take centre stage in the hangover soup, dwaeji gukbap, while in the North Chungcheong province, a type of sea snail known as olgaengi are the main ingredient in the region's hangover soup. And that's just scratching the surface of the country's many, many offerings.

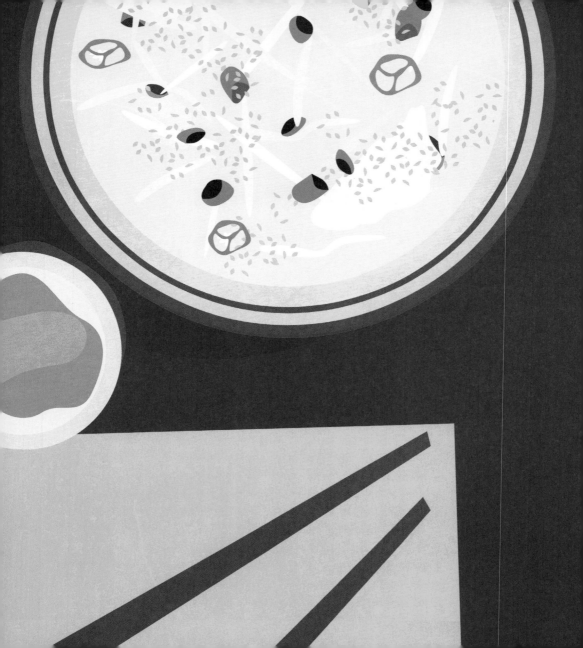

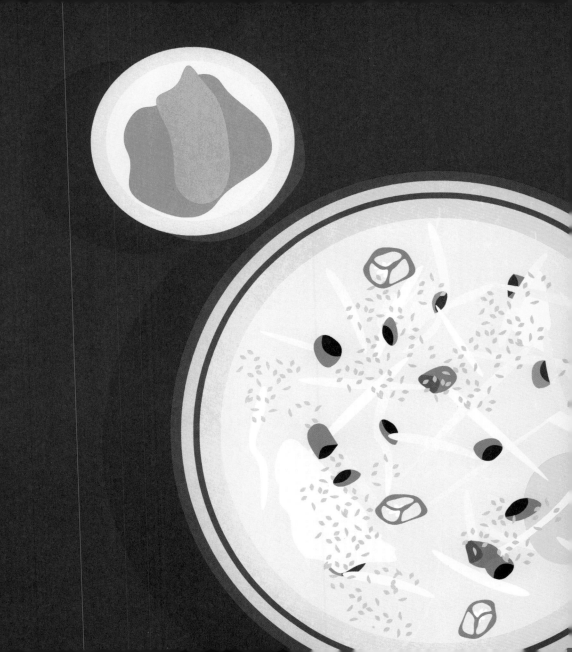

ČESNEČKA
WARMING GARLIC SOUP

CZECH REPUBLIC

SERVES 2
PREP TIME: 15 minutes
COOK TIME: 35 minutes

2 tablespoons butter

½ onion, finely chopped

3 large garlic cloves,
finely minced

200 g (7 oz) waxy potatoes,
peeled and cut into
2 cm (¾ in) cubes

½ teaspoon dried marjoram

1 bay leaf

¼ teaspoon caraway seeds

240 ml (8 fl oz/1 cup) beef stock

salt and freshly ground
black pepper

1 tablespoon chopped parsley

croutons, to serve (optional)

This garlic-laced soup is classic comfort food in the Czech Republic, not to mention a great antidote to an evening of too many Pilsners. Because it's simple and rustic, made with minimal ingredients, you'll want to use the best quality beef stock you can get your hands on. *Česnečka* is traditionally served with fried bread, and while your hangover may be telling you not to complicate the cooking process, it's well worth it to make your own croutons. Simply cut up a baguette into cubes, drizzle with several glugs of olive oil and a pinch of salt, toss to combine, and bake at 150°C (300°F/Gas 1) for about 20 minutes, or until golden brown all over. Start the croutons before prepping your other ingredients and they'll be finished just as the soup is ready to come off the stove.

HANGOVER HELPER

Look across Eastern Europe and you'll discover several other soups revered as hangover cures. In Hungary, *korhelyleves*, a robust sausage and sauerkraut soup, shocks hungover revellers back to reality, while in Russia and Ukraine, *solyanka*, a spicy, sour soup made with pickles, pickle brine (yes, there it is again!) and an arsenal of meat products, is said to knock out a hangover with gusto.

1. Melt the butter in a saucepan over medium heat. Add the onion and fry until translucent, about 5 minutes. Add the garlic and continue cooking for another minute, making sure that the garlic does not burn.
2. Add the potatoes, marjoram, bay leaf and caraway. Stir to combine, then add 360 ml (12 fl oz/1½ cups) water and the beef stock. Bring to a boil, then lower the heat to a simmer and cook, covered, until the potatoes are soft, about 15 minutes. Season to taste with salt (about ¼–½ teaspoon) and several grindings of pepper. Top with the parsley and croutons, if using (you absolutely should be using).

OCHAZUKE
GREEN TEA AND RICE SOUP

─── **JAPAN** ───

SERVES 2
PREP TIME: 15 minutes
(assuming you've already got
cooked rice in the refrigerator)

---

130 g (4½ oz/1 cup) hot, cooked
short-grain rice

50 g (1¾ oz) hot-smoked
(kippered) salmon, skin removed
and flaked into small pieces

2 pieces umeboshi (Japanese
pickled plum)

2 tablespoons thinly sliced spring
onion (scallion)

2 teaspoons crumbled or thinly
sliced nori (seaweed)

4 teaspoons bubu arare
(Japanese rice cracker balls)
or crushed plain rice crackers or
unsweetened puffed rice cereal
like Rice Krispies

500 ml (17½ fl oz/2 cups) hot
green tea

Ochazuke is the Japanese equivalent to 'kitchen sink' cuisine –
it's a dish you quickly throw together based on whatever bits
and bobs you've got leftover in the refrigerator. The only real
requirement for this traditional soup is that it must contain
green tea and rice. Use any kind of green tea (tea bags are
fine too), save for matcha, which has too strong a flavour. This
version of ochazuke is prepared with salmon and umeboshi,
which are intensely sour Japanese salted plums (they're available
online or at Japanese supermarkets). Umeboshi themselves are
also touted as a hangover cure in Japan. They're pretty mouth-
puckering, though, so spoon up with caution.

1. Divide the hot rice between two large soup bowl. Top with
   the hot-smoked salmon, umeboshi, spring onion, nori and
   bubu arare.
2. Pour 1 cup of the green tea over each bowl of rice and
   toppings and serve immediately.

CALDO DE CAMARÓN
SPICY PRAWN SOUP

MEXICO

SERVES 2
PREP TIME: 20 minutes
COOK TIME: 1 hour

---

4 dried guajillo chillies, seeded
   and stems removed

3 dried chipotle chillies, seeded
   and stems removed

3 tablespoons small dried shrimp

3 tablespoons vegetable oil

1 onion, roughly chopped

3 garlic cloves, chopped

2 tomatoes, cored and
   roughly chopped

1 teaspoon dried epazote (optional)

1 large carrot, peeled and diced

1 small potato, peeled and diced

¾ teaspoon salt

250 g (9 oz) raw prawns (shrimp),
   shelled and deveined

½ lime, cut into 2 wedges

2 tablespoons onion, minced,
   to serve

2 tablespoons coriander
   (cilantro), minced, to serve

Mexico has no shortage of hangover cures. Besides the Michelada (page 38) and Easy Chilaquiles (page 64), it's home to *vuelve a la vida* (a spicy seafood cocktail whose name literally translates as 'return to life'), *barbacoa* (meat that's been barbecued in a pit in the ground until succulent), *birria* (spicy goat stew) and Caldo de Camarón, this spicy prawn soup. The addition of *chipotle* peppers here is not traditional, but the smoky, warming flavours pair wonderfully with the prawns and vegetables. This dish is moderately spicy; if you'd like it even spicier (all the better to sweat out that hangover), add in a dried chile de arbol or two along with the guajillos and chipotles. To prepare the dried chillies, use scissors to cut the tops off, then cut down the chilli and use your fingers to brush away any seeds. Then be sure to wash your hands well – you won't be able to enjoy the soup if you've accidentally got chilli residue in your eye.

1. Bring 240 ml (8 fl oz/1 cup) of water to a boil. Place the chillies in a small bowl along with the dried shrimp. Pour the water into the bowl and let sit for 10 minutes until the chillies soften, then discard the water.

Mexico's got one other brothy bowl in its culinary catalogue of hangover remedies: *menudo*, which is a spicy tripe soup enriched with dried chillies. But it's not the only country where tripe soup is a tried and tested hangover cure. In Romania, *ciorbă de burtă* is a popular cure-all in which the tripe is cooked with root vegetables in a broth thickened with sour cream and garnished with pickled peppers. And in Turkey, the go-to hangover soup, *işkembe çorbası*, pairs tripe with a rich egg yolk-lemon juice broth.

2. While the chillies and shrimp are soaking, heat 2 tablespoons of the oil in a medium-sized saucepan over medium-high heat and fry the onion and garlic until lightly brown, about 5–7 minutes. Add the tomato and epazote, if using, followed by the soaked chillies and dried shrimp. Cook over medium heat for 5 minutes, stirring occasionally. Turn off the heat, then add 240 ml (8 fl oz/1 cup) cold water and either using a hand-held blender or a blender, whizz until smooth. Strain into a large bowl through a fine mesh sieve (strainer), using a wooden spoon to press any pulp to release the liquid. You should have about 475 ml (16 fl oz/2 cups) of the soup base.
3. Rinse and wipe out the pan (or get a new one if you're lazy) and heat the remaining 1 tablespoon oil over medium-high heat. Add the carrot and potato and fry for 1 minute. Add the soup base, salt and 240 ml (8 fl oz/1 cup) water. Bring to a boil, then turn the heat to medium-low and cook, covered, for about 20 minutes, or until the vegetables are soft.
4. Add the prawns and continue cooking, covered, until they have turned pink, about 2 minutes.
5. Ladle the soup into two bowls, squeeze over some juice from the lime wedges and top with the onion and coriander.

TARATOR
ALBANIAN CHILLED CUCUMBER SOUP

BALKANS

SERVES 2
PREP TIME: 45 minutes
(includes chilling time)

½ cucumber

350 g (12 oz/1½ cups) Greek
   yoghurt

1 tablespoon olive oil

1 medium garlic clove,
   finely minced

1 teaspoon salt

4 tablespoons dill, chopped

You'll find *tarator*, a garlic-kissed cold cucumber soup or dip, all throughout the Balkans and especially in Albania. Similar to *tzatziki*, this light, refreshing soup is often consumed in the summertime, and, interestingly, after a few too many shots of *rakia*, a fruit-based brandy popular throughout the region. If you think about it, though, cucumbers and yoghurt both have a high water content, so you're essentially rehydrating your body back to health. Note that the garlic flavour of the soup can become stronger the longer you let it sit, so if you're making it in advance of a night of drinking, you may want to go easy on the allium. Or maybe the potent garlic will be just what you need to jolt you back to clear-headedness.

1. Peel the cucumber, then slice it in half lengthways. Using a small spoon, scoop out and discard the seeds. Grate the cucumber into a large bowl.
2. Add the yoghurt, 100 ml (3½ fl oz/scant ½ cup) cold water, the oil, garlic, salt and dill and stir to combine. Refrigerate for 30 minutes, until well chilled.

FRICASÉ
HEARTY PORK STEW

BOLIVIA

SERVES 2
PREP TIME: 10 minutes
COOK TIME: 2½ hours

1 tablespoon vegetable oil

1 teaspoon salt

¼ teaspoon freshly ground
black pepper

340 g (12 oz) pork shoulder,
chopped into 5 cm (2 in) cubes

1 onion, very finely chopped

3 large garlic cloves, minced

2 tablespoons aji amarillo purée

½ teaspoon ground cumin

¼ teaspoon dried oregano

225 g (8 oz) new potatoes

250 g (9 oz) tinned hominy
corn, drained

2 tablespoons dried breadcrumbs

Stews are popular hangover cures throughout South America. Chileans, for instance, self-medicate with *paila marina*, a light seafood broth laden with clams, mussels, prawns (shrimp) and fish, while Ecuadorians opt for a fish-based stew topped with pickled onions called *encebollado*. Bolivians, though, sweat away their hangovers with *fricasé*, a spicy pork stew amped up with aji amarillo peppers. *Fricasé* is traditionally made with *chuño*, which are freeze-dried potatoes found throughout the Andes. As *chuño* are neither widely available outside of South America nor easy to prepare, I've substituted regular new potatoes here instead. However, it's worth tracking down the aji amarillo purée (available online), as the piquant, fruity peppers provide a key flavour in this bowl of cosiness.

If you're craving something even meatier than fricasé to cure your hangover, you may want to book a plane ticket to Iran to indulge in a bowl of *kaleh pacheh*. Translating as 'head and hoof soup', the broth features a whole lamb's head (brains, tongue and all) and lamb hooves simmered with onions and warming spices for hours until tender. Served with bread known as *sangak*, pickles and a squeeze of citrus, the robust, fatty soup is generally exclusively served from 3 a.m. until sometime after dawn at speciality restaurants.

1. Heat the oil in a heavy-bottomed, lidded saucepan over medium-high heat. Season the pork cubes all over with salt and pepper, and when the oil shimmers, add the pork and cook until browned, about 3 minutes, turning the cubes as needed.

2. Remove the pork from the pan and set aside. Add the onion, garlic, aji amarillo purée, cumin and oregano to the pan and cook until the onion is translucent and soft, about 3 minutes. Return the pork to the pot and stir to combine. Add 700 ml (24 fl oz/scant 3 cups) water and bring to a boil. Cover the pan with the lid, lower the heat to a simmer and cook for 1 hour. Add the potatoes to the pot and continue to cook for another hour or until the pork is fork-tender and the potatoes are fully cooked (to check, pierce one with a knife; if the potato slips off the knife, it's done). Add the hominy corn and breadcrumbs and continue cooking, uncovered, for another 5 minutes. Check the seasoning and season to taste with additional salt and pepper, then ladle into bowls to serve.

YAKA MEIN
OLD SOBER

USA (NEW ORLEANS)

SERVES 2, generously
PREP TIME: 20 minutes
COOK TIME: 2 hours and
10 minutes

---

300 g (10½ oz) stewing beef,
 fat trimmed and cut in cubes

1 tablespoon Creole seasoning
 (such as Tony Chachere's or
 Zatarain's)

1 tablespoon vegetable oil

½ small onion, peeled, with the
 root intact

500 ml (17 fl oz/2 cups) beef
 stock (ideally one that does
 not have a lot of salt)

700 ml (24 fl oz/3 cups) water

1 tablespoon soy sauce

2 teaspoons ketchup

150 g (5 oz) spaghetti

2 hard-boiled eggs, peeled
 and halved

2 large spring onions (scallions),
 thinly sliced

Tabasco or Sriracha (optional)

It shouldn't be surprising that New Orleans, home of Bourbon Street and the raucous boozefest that is Mardi Gras, has its share of culinary hangover cures. One of the most treasured is a Chinese-Creole beef noodle soup, officially called Yaka Mein and affectionally dubbed 'Old Sober'. Yet as popular as Old Sober is in The Big Easy, Yaka Mein is virtually unknown outside of New Orleans. The soup's origins are a bit murky, but it's believed that Yaka Mein, also sometimes stylised as yaka meat, yakimeat, or ya-ka-mein or even *yock* a mein, originated with the Chinese immigrants who came to Louisiana in the 19th century to work on the railroads and sugar plantations. While a few restaurants in New Orleans today serve upmarket renditions of the dish, you'll more likely find it sold in large Styrofoam cups out of the back of a pickup truck or at one of the city's many music festivals. Because the beef takes several hours to stew, it's not the easiest dish to make hungover (timesaving tip – instead of using stewing meat, substitute paper-thin slices of beef that will cook quickly, or swap out prawns (shrimp) for the beef). Or perhaps it gets its name because by the time all the cooking's done, you've gone from hungover to old sober yourself.

Head east to Tidewater Virginia, and you'll likely encounter yaka mein's distant relative, 'yock,' a dish of lo mein noodles dressed in a soy-ketchup sauce topped with chopped raw onions. It doesn't have quite the hangover-curing mythos surrounding it that yaka mein does, but I bet it'd get the job done following a long night at the pub.

1. Preheat the oven to 175°C (350°F/Gas 4). Season the beef all over with the Creole seasoning. Heat the vegetable oil in a heavy-bottomed, lidded casserole dish (Dutch oven) over medium-high heat. Add the halved onion and beef cubes and cook until browned, about 3 minutes, turning the cubes as needed.

2. Add the beef stock, water, soy sauce and ketchup to the dish and bring to a boil. Cover, then transfer to the oven and cook until the beef is fork-tender, about 1½ hours. Discard the onion, then remove the beef cubes from the casserole dish, transfer them to a cutting board and chop into small pieces. Return the beef to the dish and set aside.

3. Bring a saucepan full of salty water to the boil and cook the spaghetti according to the directions on the packet. Drain and set aside.

4. Bring the beef broth back to a boil. To serve, divide the spaghetti, beef broth and shredded beef into two bowls. Top each bowl with two hard-boiled egg halves and the spring onions. Top with Tabasco or sriracha, if desired, and serve immediately.

CHAPTER 5

SNACKS AND SANDWICHES

Sometimes, when your hangover is a real doozy and you're not ready to commit to a full-on meal, opt for the small bites and snacks at the beginning of this chapter. They're perfect for pecking and easing you into the day. However, once you've gotten over the stumbling block, you need to plan for something substantial but simple: enter sandwiches. A sandwich is, all too often, an afterthought – something you'd throw into your bag for a sad desk lunch. But in truth, a well-constructed sandwich can almost be a work of art; a perfect balance of protein, vegetables, cheese and bread. Hangover sandwiches, depending on where in the world you are, run the gamut from two-ingredient toasties to extravagant meat-stuffed beasts, yet all share a common goal of squishing satisfying ingredients between two slices of bread.

BACON BUTTY

UK

SERVES 1
PREP TIME: 5 minutes
COOK TIME: 10 minutes

4 strips thick-cut smoked streaky bacon

2 teaspoons butter, softened

2 slices white bread

2 teaspoons HP sauce (or ketchup, if you want to go against the grain)

Perhaps the greatest British sandwich of all time – and certainly the one most desired after a boozy night – is the bacon butty. Prince Harry even arranged a 'survivor's breakfast' of bacon sandwiches following Prince William and Kate Middleton's wedding. Several schools of thought clash over the definition of a perfect bacon butty. Are you team brown sauce or team ketchup? Toasted bread or untoasted? Back bacon or streaky bacon? A poll conducted a few years back determined that Brits prefer untoasted white bread with smoked bacon covered in brown sauce. After much deliberation and testing various combinations, I have to agree with the masses.

1. Place the bacon in a large frying pan over medium-high heat. After about 3 minutes, or when the edges are just starting to brown, turn the bacon and cook on the opposite side. Lower the heat slightly and continue cooking, flipping as needed, until the bacon is just beginning to crisp up, about 5 more minutes. Transfer the bacon to a paper towel to drain.
2. Meanwhile, spread the butter on one slice of the bread. Spread the HP sauce on the other slice of bread.
3. Place the bacon on the buttered bread and top with the other slice of bread, HP-side down.

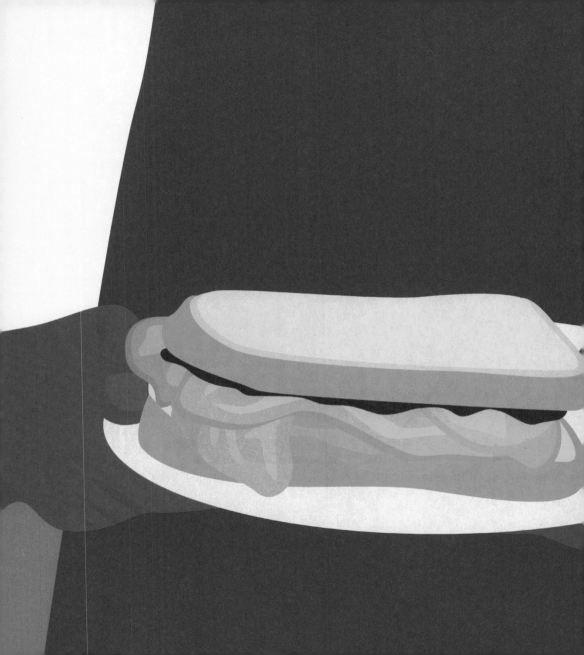

IRISH CRISP SANDWICH

SERVES 1
PREP TIME: 5 minutes

---

1 tablespoon unsalted butter, softened

2 slices soft white, thickly cut sandwich bread

1 x 35-g (1.2 oz) packet of crisps, ideally Tayto's cheese and onion flavour

For the mornings when even your hangover has a hangover, behold the crisp sandwich, a deliciously junky treat from the Emerald Isle, and equally as popular in the UK. Given the limited number of ingredients, aim for the best here. Slather some rich, creamy butter on the bounciest white bread you can get your hands on, dump a bag of crisps on top and voila, a hangover cure is served. The go-to crisps for this sandwich in Ireland are the cheese-and-onion-flavoured ones from Tayto, an Irish company credited with creating the first flavoured crisps, but in the UK, it's often salt-and-vinegar crisps or pickled onion-flavoured Monster Munch. This is neither a beautiful nor glamorous sandwich, but good God, it is glorious.

1. Spread the softened butter on each slice of bread.
2. Top one slice of the buttered bread with the crisps. Place the other piece of bread butter-side down on the crisps. Cut in half, if desired, and cradle the sandwich in your hands to avoid any crisp spillage.

FISH FINGER SANDWICH

SERVES 1
PREP TIME: 5
COOK TIME: 20 minutes

150 g (5¼ oz) chunky fish fingers
   (about 3–4 fingers depending
   on brand)
Tartare sauce (see below)
2 slices soft white sandwich bread
small handful of rocket (arugula)
   leaves

For the tartare sauce
4 tablespoons mayonnaise
4 teaspoons finely chopped
   cornichons
2 teaspoons finely chopped
   capers
1 teaspoon finely chopped dill
¼ teaspoon lemon juice
large pinch of caster (granulated)
   sugar
pinch of salt
pinch of freshly ground
   black pepper

The fish finger sandwich is one of those comfort foods that can be as humble or as posh as you'd like it to be. Many a Brit would be satisfied with a few crispy fish fingers and a swirl of ketchup or a little butter on soft white bread. On the other hand, you can now flock to restaurants for gussied up versions made with artisanal bakery buns, various kinds of fish and an array of seasonings and toppings. This rendition finds itself somewhere in the middle, punched up with freshly made tartare sauce and a handful of rocket for a spicy bite. It's easy enough to prepare when hungover, but fancy enough that you don't need to hide in shame while eating it in your pyjamas.

1. Prepare the fish fingers according to the instructions on the packet. While the fish fingers are cooking, combine all ingredients for the tartare sauce together in a small bowl.
2. Spread the tartare sauce evenly over the two slices of bread. Top one of the slices with the rocket and top with the fish fingers once they've finished cooking. Place the other slice of bread, tartare sauce-side down, on top of the fish and press down softly for a few seconds before serving.

BACON, EGG AND CHEESE SANDWICH

USA (NEW YORK CITY)

SERVES 1
PREP TIME: 5 minutes
COOK TIME: 10 minutes

---

1 Kaiser roll or crusty white bread roll

1 tablespoon butter, softened

3 slices streaky bacon, cut in half

2 eggs

pinch of salt

pinch of freshly ground black pepper

1 slice American cheese

America's answer to Britain's bacon butty is the bacon, egg and cheese sandwich, affectionately referred to as the BEC. Wrapped in shiny foil and procured from bodegas (cornershops with takeaway hot food) and street food stalls, it's the iconic breakfast sandwich that powers New York City denizens as they fight the crowds hustling to work on the subway. While fancy versions abound nowadays, any self-respecting New Yorker will concur that the BEC should feature American cheese along with either scrambled or fried eggs and be served on a Kaiser roll (a type of crusty bread roll), for this is not some fancy, schmancy, artisanal, brioche-based concoction. This is the everyman's sandwich.

1. Slice the roll in half and spread the butter on the bottom half.
2. Place the bacon in a frying pan over medium-high heat. Cook the bacon until crisp, turning occasionally, about 5–7 minutes. Remove from the frying pan, leaving the bacon fat in the pan, and place on the buttered half of the roll. Top the bacon with the cheese so the heat melts it slightly.
3. Crack the eggs into the pan and stir, breaking up the yolk. Season to taste with the salt and freshly ground black pepper, and continue cooking, stirring regularly, until the eggs are fully cooked, about another minute or two. If you don't like scrambled eggs, you can fry them instead.
4. Place the eggs on top of the cheese. Place the other half of the roll on top, pressing for a few seconds so the heat of the eggs melts the cheese. Enjoy immediately.

WAFFLE IRON HASH BROWNS

USA

SERVES 2
PREP TIME: 15 minutes
COOK TIME: 10 minutes

---

2 large russet or maris piper potatoes, peeled and grated

1½ teaspoons salt

½ teaspoon freshly ground black pepper

4 tablespoons butter, melted

Salty and starchy, hash browns are a popular diner staple around the USA and unquestionably a feature of many a hungover American's breakfast plate. While normally prepared on a plancha or in a frying pan, hash browns get an upgrade when made in a waffle iron, as the surface area of potential crispy bits is maximised. As every waffle maker is different, you'll want to keep an eye on the waffle as it's cooking. When it's done, you should be able to remove it in one solid, crispy, crunchy piece.

Hash browns aren't the only food you can hack a waffle iron to make. After achieving success with shredded spuds, try whipping up the following dishes:

- Brownies (prepare batter as normal, then cook until set)
- Falafel (make chickpea mixture, then cook until the patties are crispy)
- Quesadillas (sprinkle a tortilla with loads of cheese, top with another tortilla and press until crisp)
- Bacon (Lay slices of bacon in the waffle maker, moving as needed to ensure all areas get crisp)
- Macaroni and cheese (place leftover cooked mac and cheese in the iron and heat until crispy and hot)
- Veggie omelettes (whisk some eggs with cooked veg of your choice, then pour into the waffle maker and heat until set)

While delicious eaten plain, a hash brown waffle is a blank canvas.

Here are some of my favourite toppings:

- Fried eggs and hot sauce
- Salsa, sour cream and grated Cheddar
- Ketchup. Lots of ketchup.
- Melted Cheddar and broccoli
- Poached eggs and hollandaise sauce
- Sour cream and apple sauce
- Baked beans
- Chilli con carne
- Caramelised onions and fried mushrooms

1. Preheat your waffle iron according to the manufacturer's instructions.
2. Tip the grated potatoes into a bowl. Add the salt, pepper and 2 tablespoons melted butter and mix until well combined.
3. Working handful by handful, squeeze out any excess liquid from the potato mixture. Set the potatoes on a paper towel for a few seconds to absorb any additional liquid.
4. Grease the waffle iron with the remaining melted butter. Place the potatoes in the waffle iron in an even layer and close the iron. You should be able to make around four waffles. Cook on medium heat until golden brown all over and the waffle easily lifts out, about 8–10 minutes, checking the waffle from time to time to make sure it's not burning. Serve immediately.

THREE-MEAT SANDWICH

PUERTO RICO

SERVES 1, generously
PREP TIME: 10 minutes
COOK TIME: 30 minutes
(including marinating time)

---

110 g (4 oz) skirt steak

2 tablespoons olive oil

1 teaspoon red wine vinegar

1 teaspoon Goya Adobo
   seasoning

1 tablespoon ketchup

1 tablespoon mayonnaise

85 g (3 oz) sliced deli ham,
   roughly chopped

85 g (3 oz) sliced deli chicken,
   chopped

1 soft mini baguette or white
   bread roll, halved

1 small tomato, cored and
   thinly sliced

35 g (1¼ oz) shredded
   iceberg lettuce

20 g (¾ oz) potato sticks (or
   crushed lightly salted crisps,
   if unavailable, crushed)

Internet folklore says that Puerto Ricans will rub half a lemon under their armpits prior to a night of drinking to help prevent dehydration. I've yet to encounter anyone who's tried this, let alone anyone who will vouch for its efficacy. However, a hearty sandwich called the *tripleta*, so named because it stuffs three different types of meats between soft bread, is a confirmed hangover cure on the streets of San Juan. The variations abound, and you may encounter some filled with *pernil* (slow-roasted pork) or topped with cheese, but often you'll find a mix of chicken, ham and steak. This version comes together fairly quickly thanks to pre-purchased, sliced meat.

1. Using a mallet, pound the skirt steak as thinly as possible (think paper-thin), then cut the meat into bite-sized pieces. Place the steak pieces in a resealable plastic bag or a bowl along with the olive oil, red wine vinegar and Goya Adobo seasoning, stir to combine, and let marinate for 15 minutes.
2. While the steak is marinating, combine the ketchup and mayonnaise together in a small bowl and set aside.
3. Heat a frying pan over high heat, then add the steak and its marinade and fry until the steak pieces are fully cooked and the edges are just starting to crisp up, about 2 minutes.

Puerto Rico's (and really, much of the rest of Latin America's) other beloved hangover cure is *sancocho*, a stew rich with starchy vegetables such as yucca, potatoes, pumpkin, corn and plantains. Beef is commonly used in Puerto Rico, though as you work your way down to Panama and Colombia, chicken becomes the primary protein source in the soup.

4. Turn the heat off. Add the ham and chicken to the frying pan, stirring until combined and the meats are warmed through. Remove the pan from the heat.
5. To assemble the sandwich, slather the ketchup-mayonnaise sauce on both halves of the baguette or roll. Spoon the meat onto the bottom half, then top with the lettuce, tomato and potato sticks. Top with the remaining half of the baguette, sauce-side down, and press gently on the sandwich to secure everything in place. Serve immediately.

VEGEMITE AND AVOCADO TOAST

SERVES 1
PREP TIME: 5 minutes
COOK TIME: 5 minutes

---

*1 large slice sourdough or
    white bread*
1 teaspoon butter, softened
1 teaspoon Vegemite
*½ large avocado or
    1 small avocado*
*large pinch of freshly ground
    black pepper*
large pinch of chilli flakes
1 teaspoon lemon juice

A heavy night of drinking depletes the body of many of its essential nutrients, particularly the B vitamins. However, Australia's popular spread, Vegemite, is chock full of B vitamins, making it one of the reasons Aussies consider Vegemite on toast to be the ideal hangover food. If you don't come from the land Down Under (which dictates that your kitchen cupboard be stocked with Vegemite at all times), you can easily acquire it online. Be warned, though – made from brewer's yeast, Vegemite has a strong, malty, soy sauce-like flavour that people either love or hate. If the classic Vegemite on toast is too hard to stomach, try it first as the base for another Aussie favourite, avocado toast.

1. Toast the bread in a toaster or under the grill (broiler) until golden brown.
2. Spread the butter on the bread in an even layer.
3. Spread the Vegemite on top of the butter in an even layer. Enjoy as is, or proceed to step 4 to make the avocado toast version.
4. Scoop out the flesh from the avocado in a bowl. Add the freshly ground black pepper, the chilli flakes and the lemon juice and mash with a fork until chunky. Spoon the avocado purée on top of the buttered, Vegemited toast and serve.

FRANCESINHA
PORTUGUESE HANGOVER SANDWICH

PORTUGAL (PORTO)

SERVES 1, very generously
PREP TIME: 15 minutes
COOK TIME: 45 minutes

For the sauce

2 tablespoons olive oil

½ small onion, chopped

1 large garlic clove, chopped

1 bay leaf

½ teaspoon chilli flakes

1 teaspoon cornflour (cornstarch)

2 tablespoons port

2 tablespoons brandy

60 ml (2 fl oz/¼ cup) beef stock

250 ml (8½ fl oz/1 cup) light lager

80 ml (2¾ fl oz/⅓ cup) passata
(tomato purée)

½ teaspoon Worcestershire sauce

1 tablespoon double (heavy)
cream

salt

continued on next page

A speciality from the city of Porto, the *francesinha* is essentially the Portuguese riff on the classic French *croque monsieur*, albeit one taken to the extreme. The decadent, artery-clogging sandwich is stuffed with a selection of meats, smothered in cheese and drowned in a tomato sauce enriched with port, brandy and beer (timesaving tip: you can easily prepare the sauce in advance of being hungover). If you can't find linguiça, a traditional Portuguese sausage spiked with paprika, substitute the more widely available Spanish chorizo, French andouille or even Polish kielbasa. The sandwich is often served with French fries and a beer, because, well, if you're really looking to cure that hangover, you might as well go big or go home.

1. First, prepare the sauce: in a medium-sized saucepan, heat the olive oil over medium-high heat. Add the onion, garlic, bay leaf and chilli flakes and cook until the onion has softened, about 3–5 minutes.
2. Sprinkle over the cornflour, stirring until combined. Add the port and brandy and cook, stirring occasionally, until the alcohol has evaporated, about 2 minutes.
3. Add the beef stock, beer, passata and Worcestershire sauce and raise the heat to high. Cook at a rolling boil for about 10 minutes, or until the mixture has reduced by about half, has thickened and is sauce-like. Add the cream and stir until combined. Strain into a bowl or small jug, and season to taste with salt. Set aside.

HANGOVER HELPER

For the sandwich

1 tablespoon olive oil

2 small pork sausages, such as
  chipolatas

50 g (2 oz) linguiça, chorizo,
  andouille or kielbasa sausage,
  thinly sliced

2 slices white sandwich bread

2 slices ham

2 slices roast beef

3 slices Swiss cheese, such as
  Emmental or Gruyère

1 egg

4. Prepare the sandwich fillings while the sauce is reducing: heat the olive oil in a non-stick frying pan over medium-high heat. Add the pork sausages and cook, turning occasionally, until almost done, about 8–10 minutes. Add the cured sausage to the pan and cook until the edges are beginning to brown, about 2 minutes. Remove the sausages from the frying pan, leaving the fat in the pan and keeping the frying pan on the hob as you'll use it again shortly. Cut the whole sausages in half lengthways.

5. Turn a grill (broiler) to high. Toast the two slices of bread on a foil-lined baking (cookie) sheet until lightly golden brown. Top one slice of bread with the ham, roast beef and both types of sausages. Top with the other piece of bread, then cover the sandwich in the cheese slices so that it is fully draped in cheese.

6. Heat the frying pan that you cooked the sausages in over medium-high heat. Crack an egg into it and cook sunny-side up, so that the whites are firm and the yolk is runny, about 2 minutes. Set aside.

7. Transfer the baking sheet with the sandwich to the grill and cook until the cheese is fully melted, about 1–2 minutes.

8. To serve, transfer the sandwich to a plate and top with the egg. Pour the sauce over the sandwich, letting the sauce pool on the plate (there may be a little sauce leftover). Serve immediately.

CHILLI CHEESE TOAST

INDIA

SERVES 1
PREP TIME: 10 minutes
COOK TIME: 10 minutes

1 slice white bread

1 tablespoon butter, softened

30 g (1 oz/⅓ cup) grated mild Cheddar

2 tablespoons shredded low-moisture mozzarella cheese

1 teaspoon very finely chopped red onion

1 tablespoon very finely chopped coriander (cilantro)

2 tablespoons finely chopped jalapeño chilli

¼ teaspoon mustard powder

pinch of salt

generous pinch of freshly ground black pepper

It's been proven that a soft, bubbling blanket of melted cheese on bread eases a hangover as much as being wrapped in bed in a blanket of the finest cashmere – which is to say, quite a lot. Chilli cheese toast, also a favourite food among Indian school children, is often made with processed Amul cheese, but this version uses a combination of the more widely available Cheddar and mozzarella. One toast will suffice for a hearty snack, but it isn't quite enough to make a full meal. Double the recipe if you need fortification, or, in the manner of turning anything into a delicious breakfast dish, simply put an egg on it

1. Preheat the oven to 200°C (400°F/Gas 6).
2. Spread the butter evenly on one side of the bread. Place the bread butter-side up on a foil-lined baking (cookie) sheet and bake until lightly golden on the bottom, about 5 minutes.
3. Meanwhile, combine all the remaining ingredients in a bowl.
4. Remove the baking sheet from the oven and spread the cheese mixture in an even layer across the toast. Return to the oven and continue cooking until the cheese is fully melted, about 5 minutes. Serve immediately.

Craving the flavours of India to cure your hangover but not in the mood for chilli cheese toast? Another popular Indian hangover breakfast is a masala omelette, studded with chopped green chillies, onion, tomato, coriander (cilantro) and Indian spices.

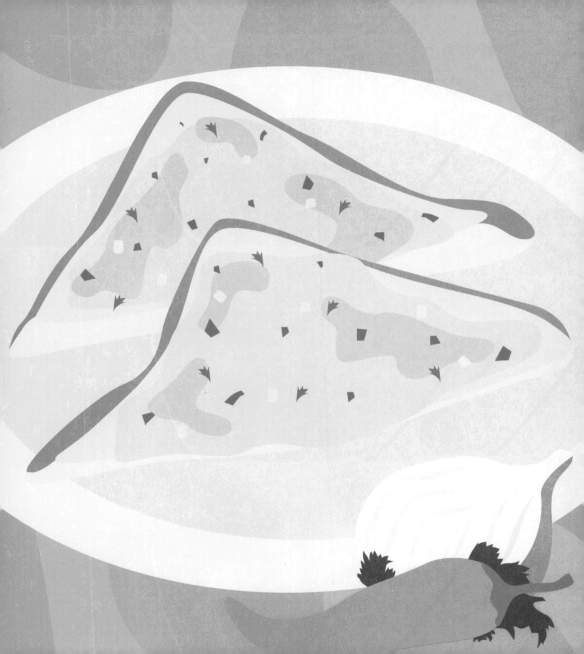

BEAVER TAILS

CANADA

SERVES 2 generously (makes 6 pieces)
PREP TIME: 5 minutes
COOK TIME: 1 hour and 15 minutes (includes resting time)

For the beaver tails

2 tablespoons plus ¼ teaspoon granulated sugar

1 teaspoon fast-action dried yeast

salt

1 litre (4 cups) vegetable oil

140 g (5 oz/1 cup plus 2 tablespoons) flour, plus extra for dusting

50 g (2 oz/⅓ cup) wholemeal (wholewheat) flour

For the topping

200 g (7 oz/scant 1 cup) caster (granulated) sugar

2 teaspoons ground cinnamon

Fear not, you won't be required to kill and skin any dam-building rodents in order to enjoy chowing down on beaver tails. Rather, beaver tails are hand-stretched, deep-fried discs of dough, often topped with cinnamon and sugar. First invented in the late 1970s in Ottawa, Canada, beaver tails have since become the namesake item of a national chain with 124 locations across Canada. While most associated with country fairs, ice skating rinks and nourishing those après-ski hunger pangs, the oblong-shaped treat (hence the name) also makes for a delicious hangover snack when you're yearning for something crispy and sugary. I also like to consider them the sweeter, long-lost twin of one of Hungary's favourite hangover foods, *lángos*: deep-fried yeasted dough topped with cheese, ham, garlic and myriad other savoury toppings.

1. Place 2 tablespoons warm water, the ¼ teaspoon of the sugar and the yeast in the bowl of a stand mixer. Let sit for about 5 minutes, or until the mixture is foamy. Add a pinch of salt, 115 ml (4 fl oz/½ cup) water, the remaining 2 tablespoons sugar and 2 teaspoons vegetable oil to the mixer. Mix on low speed until combined. Add the flours and mix until fully incorporated. The dough will be very sticky but pulling apart from the sides of the bowl slightly. Form the dough into a ball and place in the bottom of the mixing bowl. Cover the mixing bowl with cling film (plastic wrap), then place in a slightly warm area (an oven that's turned off and completely cool, for instance, or above the refrigerator) and let sit for about 30–40 minutes, or until the dough doubles in size.

Cinnamon sugar is a classic when it comes to beaver tail toppings, but there's no need to stop there. Experiment with any of the following sweet options, Canadian-style, make it more like lángos with savoury options, or let your hungover imagination run wild.

Sweet
- Nutella and banana slices
- Maple butter and chocolate sauce
- Apple butter, apple slices and caramel sauce
- Vanilla buttercream icing and crushed Oreos
- Biscoff spread, whipped cream and butterscotch pieces

Savoury
- Garlic butter
- Sour cream, ham, shaved onions and grated cheese
- Crème fraîche, smoked salmon, caviar and chopped dill
- Ranch dressing, crumbled crispy streaky bacon and pickled jalapeño slices
- Pesto, roasted tomatoes and crumbled goat's cheese

2. While the dough is resting, prepare the topping by mixing the sugar and cinnamon together on a plate or flat, shallow bowl until combined.

3. Generously sprinkle a clean work surface with flour, then take the dough and, using your hands, flatten and stretch it into six tail-shaped pieces, roughly 25 x 8 cm (10 x 3 in). You want the dough to be as thin as possible without tearing. If it tears, just press it back together with your fingers.

4. Heat the remaining vegetable oil in a heavy-bottomed saucepan over high heat until the oil reaches 175°C (350°F). Add two of the beaver tails to the oil and deep-fry, using tongs to flip occasionally, until they are dark golden brown on both sides, about 1½ minutes in total. If you see any air pockets forming in the dough, use the tongs to gently press out the air while submerged in the oil.

5. Remove the beaver tails from the oil using the tongs and immediately transfer to the bowl of cinnamon sugar. Working quickly, coat them in the cinnamon sugar (you may need to use both hands for this, pressing the sugar against the dough) and then transfer to a plate.

6. Repeat with the remaining beaver tails, then serve immediately.

HERRING ROLLMOPS

SERVES 2 as a snack or as part of a larger hangover breakfast
PREP TIME: 5 minutes

2 pickled herring fillets
4 cornichons
1 tablespoon thinly sliced onion

The German language is filled with many glorious, untranslatable words, several of them related to drinking culture. There's *schnapsidee*, or 'schnapps idea', which roughly translates to a stupid idea that seemed great when you were drunk (or, conversely, an idea so stupid that it must have come from a place of drunkenness). Then you've got *die alkoholleiche*, or 'the alcohol corpse', which refers to someone who's passed out from drinking too much. And finally, there's the *katerfrühstück*, otherwise known as a 'hangover breakfast'. Rollmops, or pickled herring wrapped around pickles and onions, are a traditional part of the katerfrühstück and are full of the vitamins and salts your body craves after a night of drinking. They're a bit of an acquired taste on their own, so serve alongside some buttered brown bread, hard-boiled eggs, a few slices of cheese and a steaming pot of herbal tea.

1. Slice each herring fillet in half widthways.
2. Carefully roll each herring fillet around one cornichon and a few pieces of thinly sliced onion. Secure in place with a toothpick and serve

BEANS ON TOAST

UK

SERVES 2
PREP TIME: 5 minutes
COOK TIME: 10 minutes

1 x 415 g (14½ oz) tin Heinz Beanz
2 slices white or sourdough bread
2 teaspoons butter, softened
2 tablespoons grated mature
   Cheddar (optional)

Everyone knows the only proper way to make beans on toast is to pull out a tin of Heinz and a loaf of bread from the pantry. It is a dish whose simplicity belies its supremacy in the rankings of the best of British cuisine. Should you want to challenge yourself while hungover, though, you can recreate a pretty similar version using dried beans. You'll need to start the process before you start drinking, though, as the beans require a good soak overnight.

THE EASY WAY

1. Pour the beans into a saucepan and cook over medium-high heat until the beans are bubbling and hot.
2. Toast the bread in a toaster or under the grill (broiler) until golden brown. Remove and spread 1 teaspoon butter on each slice of bread.
3. Place the toast on two plates and top with the beans. Sprinkle with the Cheddar, if using, and serve immediately.

SERVES 2
PREP TIME: 10 minutes
COOK TIME: 1 hour and 10 minutes, plus soaking overnight

---

90 g (3¼ oz/½ cup) dried cannellini or great northern beans

½ teaspoon salt

¼ teaspoon garlic powder

¾ teaspoon onion powder

¼ teaspoon ground mustard

2 teaspoons sugar

80 ml (2¾ fl oz/⅓ cup) passata (tomato purée)

1 tablespoon apple cider vinegar

2 slices white or sourdough bread

2 teaspoons butter

2 tablespoons grated mature Cheddar (optional)

THE HARD WAY

1. Place the beans in a large bowl and cover with about 700 ml (24 fl oz/3 cups) cold water. Soak overnight. Drain the beans and place them in a small-to-medium-sized saucepan. Cover the beans with 500 ml (17 fl oz/2 cups) water so that the beans are fully covered. Add the salt, garlic powder, onion powder, mustard and sugar, and bring to a boil.

2. Cover and lower the heat to a gentle simmer. Cook, covered, until the beans are almost fully cooked, about 45 minutes.

3. Remove the cover and add the passata and vinegar to the pan. Stir briefly to combine. Raise the heat to medium-high and continue cooking, uncovered, until the sauce has reduced and thickened and the beans are soft, about another 10 minutes. Avoid stirring too much, as this will break the beans and you'll end up with a mushy mess.

4. Toast the bread in a toaster or under the grill (broiler) until golden brown. Remove and spread 1 teaspoon butter on each slice of bread.

5. Place the toast on two plates and top with the beans. Sprinkle with the Cheddar, if using, and serve immediately.

SAUSAGE ROLLS

SERVES 2
PREP TIME: 25 minutes
COOK TIME: 25 minutes

200 g (7 oz) all-butter puff pastry
   (defrosted if frozen)
250 g (9 oz) pork sausages
2 tablespoons panko
   breadcrumbs
1 egg

Meat encased in pastry is exalted around the world for its hangover curing ability. New Zealand has its Mince and Cheese Pies (page 92) while the Balkans are home to *börek*, flaky pastries stuffed with either mild cheese or meat. Brazil, meanwhile, dishes up the *pastel*, a deep-fried, beef-filled treat for those foggy-headed mornings. The Commonwealth is home to the humble sausage roll. Buying a sausage roll from the hot counter at the supermarket is the fastest way to go from hungover to happy, but making your own is actually easier than you'd expect. Simply stock up on your favourite pork sausage (chicken, lamb and vegetarian sausages are – to be honest – sacrilege, but if it's a question of blasphemous sausage roll or no sausage roll at all, clearly blasphemous sausage wins). Then wrap it up in some shop-bought puff pastry and pop it in the oven. And in the time it takes to shower and get dressed, you've got a piping hot sausage roll on the table.

1. Preheat the oven to 200°C (400°F/Gas 6).
2. Working quickly so that the dough does not stick, roll out the puff pastry into two rectangles on a sheet of parchment paper, leaving about 10 cm (4 in) between the two rectangles. Each rectangle should be about 20 x 10 cm (8 x 4 in). Transfer the baking parchment to a baking (cookie) sheet.
3. Whisk the egg in a small dish.

Living a carb-free life but still looking to indulge in sausage-based hangover fare? Try *utopenci*, Czech 'drowning men' pickled sausages. The popular pub fare is purported to be a great cure for the morning after.

4. Squeeze the sausage meat from its casing into a bowl. Add the panko breadcrumbs and, using your hands, gently mix to combine. Shape the meat into two long logs just less than the length of the pastry. Place each sausage log lengthways on the bottom half of each pastry rectangle. Using a pastry brush or a small spoon, spread enough egg wash to cover any exposed bits of pastry. Fold the pastry over the sausage so it is now encased in dough, using your fingers to seal the dough in place. Use the tines of a fork to press down along the edges to secure the dough in place. Lightly prick the dough all over with the fork, making sure not to pierce the sausage.

5. Brush the egg wash all over the outside of the sausage rolls.

6. Bake the two logs for 25 minutes, or until well-browned. Remove from the oven, transfer to a rack and let cool slightly, at least 10 minutes, before serving. Serve hot, warm or at room temperature.

AÇAÍ NA TIGELA
AÇAÍ BOWL

BRAZIL

SERVES 1
PREP TIME: 5 minutes

1 banana

2 x 100 g (3½ oz) pouches frozen
   açaí pulp (preferably with
   guarana), slightly thawed
   and broken into chunks

2 tablespoons granola

Full of potassium and a bevy
of vitamins, it's no wonder
that bananas have a rep for
being nature's paracetamol
(Tylenol). While much hangover
food around the world utilises
ripe, sweet bananas, Uganda's
national hangover dish, *katogo*,
showcases green bananas called
matooke. Similar in flavour
and texture to plantains, the
matooke are cooked and mashed
before being topped with a
spiced beef offal stew.

The best Brazilian hangover cure is found not on a plate but in
a shiny, gold foil-wrapped packet at the pharmacy. Engov is
an over-the-counter medicine that Brazilians swear by before
hitting the clubs. Take one pill before drinking and another post-
partying and it's said you'll wake up clear-headed and ready for
a round of Caipirinhas on the beach. If you can't get your hands
on any Engov, though, *açaí na tigela*, otherwise known as an
açaí bowl, is the next best thing as it's full of antioxidants and
vitamins and is hydrating to boot. Brazilian açaí bowls are also
often sweetened with guarana syrup, which has a mild stimulant
effect, helping to further zap one's fatigue and sluggishness.
If your frozen açaí pulp isn't made with guarana, you can just
chase your açaí bowl with a strong espresso for similar results.
Likewise, while this bowl is traditional (some may say sparse) in
its toppings, feel free to modernise it with sliced strawberries,
blueberries, diced mango, toasted coconut shavings, chia seeds,
cocoa nibs, bee pollen, crushed nuts or whatever else takes
your fancy.

1. Cut the banana in half. Cut one half into slices and set
   aside. Toss the other half into a blender along with 3
   tablespoons water and the frozen açaí chunks. Blend until fully
   incorporated and the mixture has the texture of soft sorbet.
2. Transfer the mixture to a bowl, spreading it evenly with a
   spoon so the surface is flat. Top with the sliced banana and
   sprinkle with the granola. Serve immediately.

HANGOVER HELPER

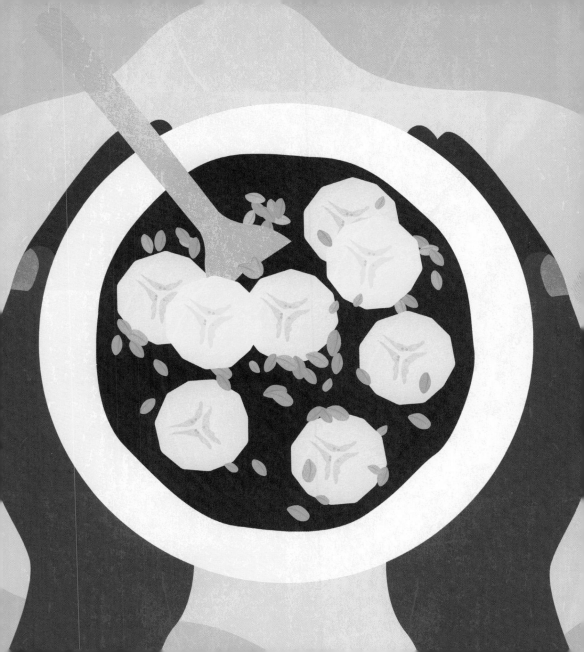

MY FAVOURITE BREAKFAST SANDWICH

SERVES 1
PREP TIME: 10 minutes
COOK TIME: 15 minutes

3 slices peppered streaky bacon,
  or plain streaky bacon
  if you can't find it

3 large prawns (shrimp),
  shelled, deveined and sliced
  in half lengthways

2 eggs

2 tablespoons sweet Thai
  chilli sauce

1 crusty mini baguette or
  submarine-style roll

5 g (¼ oz) coriander (cilantro)

I wish there were a good back story for my go-to hangover sandwich, but in truth, it's simply a few delicious ingredients cobbled together in a crusty baguette. It's my comfort, my cosiness, my indulgence, which, at the end of the day, is what hangover food is all about – getting you over the hurdle to the next hour. One word of caution – be careful biting into the sandwich as the last thing you want is a burst of burning-hot egg yolk splattering down your face. Trust me, been there, done that, and it's no fun at all. Maybe even worse than being hungover.

1. Place the bacon in a non-stick frying pan and cook over medium heat, turning until the fat has rendered from the meat and the bacon is brown and crisping at the edges, about 5–6 minutes. Leaving the fat in the pan, remove the meat and set aside on a paper towel.
2. Add the prawns to the pan with the bacon fat. Cook on each side for about 2 minutes or until firm in texture and just starting to brown. Remove the prawns and set aside on the paper towel with the bacon.
3. Crack the eggs into the pan. Once the whites have set completely, flip the eggs over using a spatula and cook for another 30 seconds just so the yolk sets but is still runny inside.
4. Spread the chilli sauce on both sides of the roll and place the coriander leaves on the bottom half. When the eggs are cooked, slide them onto the roll on top of the coriander, tucking in any loose edges falling off the sides of the bread. Top with the bacon, followed by the prawns and secure in place with the top of the roll. Serve immediately.

INDEX

THANK YOU

While writing can be a solitary endeavour, actually getting a book out in the world is very much a group effort. I couldn't have created Hangover Helper without many talented, wonderful people.

Thanks first to Molly Ahuja for your insightful editing and helping produce the hangover cookbook of my dreams. Much gratitude as well to Eila Purvis and the rest of the Hardie Grant team.

To Michelle Noel and everyone at Studio Noel, thank you for your design chops and bringing my words to life on the page.

To Sophie Melissa, thank you for all of the lovely illustrations. Hangover food has never looked more beautiful or fun to eat!

Thanks to Jenni Ferrari-Adler and the staff at Union Literary for believing in the potential of a hangover foods cookbook.

Many, many people helped me out by offering suggestions for go-to hangover dishes and drunk foods around the world. These include: Katia Grechukhina, Stephanie Bourgeois, Coreen Kopper, Marc Siegel and Maria Cruz Lopez, Tina Carletto, Carole and Andrea Rogerson, Brian Spencer, Alainna Lynch, Emmanuel Bibangamba, Fabio Parasecoli, Lotus Subhapholsiri, Kibum Kim, Jeein Ha, Jin Young Moon, Soyeon Park,

Emily Pickerill, Pegah Jalali, Adam Gurwitz, Flavia Kruschewsky, Mitchell Müller, Jess Ng, Tracy Yuen, Pamela Gross Morozini, Roberta Manco, Elizabeth Anderson, Mark Scott, Beverley Taam, Tim Tsui, Victoria Madouros, Azeem Zainulbhai, Pankil Shah, Cristina Feith, Jenn Sembler, Angie Scarlett-Newcomen, Rodolfo Longo, Robert Szulc, Andrea Monge, Alisa Richter, Daniel Vo, Melanie and Douglas MacKinnon, Scarlett Lindeman, Hajnalka Asztalos, Andras Pokorny and Nisreen Awad. Special thanks goes to Yasmin Fahr who not only made delicious beaver tails but who also first introduced me to Molly.

ABOUT THE AUTHOR

Lauren Shockey is a food writer and cook whose first book, *Four Kitchens*, recounted the year she spent learning to cook in restaurants in New York, Hanoi, Tel Aviv and Paris. Formerly the restaurant critic at *The Village Voice*, she has written for print and online publications including *The New York Times*, *The Wall Street Journal*, *Travel + Leisure*, *Saveur*, *Slate* and many more. She lives in New York City with her husband and son. Say hello to her online at www.laurenshockey.com or @LDShockey.

Hangover Helper

Published in 2019 by Hardie Grant Books,
an imprint of Hardie Grant Publishing

Hardie Grant Books (London)
5th & 6th Floors
52–54 Southwark Street
London SE1 1UN

Hardie Grant Books (Melbourne)
Building 1, 658 Church Street
Richmond, Victoria 3121

hardiegrantbooks.com

Text © Lauren Shockey
Illustrations © Sophie Melissa
Spot Illustrations © Studio Noel

British Library Cataloguing-in-Publication Data. A catalogue record for this book is available from the British Library.

ISBN: 978-1-78488-259-4

Publishing Director: Kate Pollard
Commissioning Editor: Molly Ahuja
Junior Editor: Eila Purvis
Internal and Cover Design: Studio Noel
Internal and Hero Illustrations: Sophie Melissa
Spot Illustrations: Studio Noel
Copy Editor: Eve Marleau
Proofreader: Kay Delves
Indexer: Cathy Heath
Colour Reproduction by p2d
Printed and bound in China by Leo Paper Products Ltd.